The
Category
Creation
Formula

Kevin Maney and Mike Damphousse

HARPER
BUSINESS
An Imprint of HarperCollinsPublishers

The Category Creation Formula

DISCOVER, DESIGN, AND WIN NEW MARKET CATEGORIES

THE CATEGORY CREATION FORMULA. Copyright © 2026 by Kevin Maney and Michael Damphousse. All rights reserved. Printed in the United States of America. No part of this book may be used or reproduced in any manner whatsoever without written permission except in the case of brief quotations embodied in critical articles and reviews. For information, address HarperCollins Publishers, 195 Broadway, New York, NY 10007. In Europe, HarperCollins Publishers, Macken House, 39/40 Mayor Street Upper, Dublin 1, D01 C9W8, Ireland.

HarperCollins books may be purchased for educational, business, or sales promotional use. For information, please email the Special Markets Department at SPsales@harpercollins.com.

hc.com

FIRST EDITION

Library of Congress Cataloging-in-Publication Data has been applied for.

ISBN 978-0-06-348377-4

25 26 27 28 29 LBC 5 4 3 2 1

From Kevin: This book is dedicated to my granddaughters, Susie and Mary—the newest generation. Here's hoping they live in a world of enduring positive change driven by great new companies.

From Mike: Dedicated to my wife, Linda, and our family, which continues to grow. This book is a testament to my daughters Rebecca, Carolyn, and Melissa, their husbands, and our grandkids—may this inspire you all to always challenge yourselves and deliver.

Contents

Introduction

In 2014, I began working on a book with Al Ramadan, Christopher Lochhead, and Dave Peterson—a book we ultimately ended up calling *Play Bigger: How Pirates, Dreamers, and Innovators Create and Dominate Markets.*

When we started, we had a bunch of compelling but disparate and often unconnected ideas around creating new market categories—a "bag of doorknobs," to reference a phrase from the book. But as we worked through the ideas and wrote some of the early chapters, we all felt like we were fitting together the pieces of a new business discipline.

Months into our work, the four of us gathered at Chris's house in Santa Cruz, California, which had become our book-writing headquarters. I laid out printouts and Post-its of concepts and chapter headings on Chris's enormous dining room table, lining them up like a storyboard. Al stared at the papers and Post-its and said this all reminded him of when he was a leader at Macromedia and the company created the discipline of "experience design."

After a silence, someone—Al and Chris credit me, though I don't actually remember, so who knows—said something like, "Holy shit! It's *category design!*"

I think all four of us got goosebumps. That was what we were creating. Category design would be a new discipline that would help companies identify, define, develop, and ultimately win new market categories. The key to doing all of that would be to intentionally *design* the category—design it in a way that would put a company in the driver's seat of the category. And our book was going to lay out how to do that, step by step.

Play Bigger came out in the summer of 2016. We thought we had produced something terrific, but you never know if a book is going to catch the zeitgeist. Sales started out small but steady, and then just kept going and going. Venture capitalists were handing the book out to portfolio CEOs. Founders read it and told other founders they had to read it. Marketers caught on and began changing their titles to Category Designer. And companies wanted us to help them do what we wrote about.

By the end of 2016, with a nudge from Chris, Al, and Dave, I'd formed Category Design Advisors (CDA) with Mike Damphousse, who had known and worked with *Play Bigger*'s other coauthors longer than I had. From then until this writing, Mike and I worked on category design projects for nearly fifty companies, and guided workshops for dozens more at incubators and VC portfolio gatherings. We led category design projects all over the world, through up and down economic cycles, and through a pandemic. We're working on category design today as new generations of artificial intelligence (AI) open up ways to create new market categories in every corner of business and life.

Through all that, as Mike and I put category design concepts into practice, we learned a ton. While most of *Play Bigger* was prescient and on target, we learned that there is much more to category design than we covered in that book.

Some of what we've since developed expands on the theoretical ideas behind category design. Some of it enhances the discipline's hands-on, practical aspects. We've learned that there are better ways to do some of the things in the book, like how to write a category point of view (POV) and how to roll out a category and make it stick. We developed a model for doing category design in a condensed sprint.

All of that, we feel, moves up the discipline to a higher plane. We now call what we do *strategic category design*.

This book is about what we've learned and how you, too, can practice and benefit from strategic category design. Yes, we're giving away our institutional knowledge. (Well, sort of—you probably had to pay for this book.) We believe this is bigger than us. By open-sourcing the details and secrets of strategic category design, many more companies, organizations, and individuals can benefit from it than we could ever touch as a firm. If the contents of this book help make some of them stronger, better, more meaningful, and more enduring, we all win.

And while this intro is by me—Kevin—the rest of what you'll read is by both Mike and me.

—Kevin Maney, New York, 2025

The
Category
Creation
Formula

1

The Power of Strategic Category Design

Let's begin with the end in mind.[1] As a way to tee up everything in this book, it seems like a good idea to let you in on how a strategic category design project works and how it can transform a company. We'll do this with help from the experience of one of our past clients, Prescryptive Health.

From 1999 to 2004, Chris Blackley was CEO of a company called Avao, which developed software for running retail pharmacies. After that company got acquired, he joined Microsoft and became a senior director. But he kept his eye on the pharmacy space and its convoluted, opaque, and illogical (at least to consumers) way of pricing drugs. The chief problem, Chris believed, was a type of company called a pharmacy benefits manager. These PBMs are middlemen who negotiate prescription drug prices with payers, and they usually drive up the cost of drugs and make it hard for consumers to shop for a drug based on price. Chris thought that cloud-based technology could displace PBMs, make drug pricing transparent, and help consumers get better deals.

To do just that, in 2017 Chris left Microsoft and cofounded Prescryptive with another Microsoft veteran, Kevin Young. They had a big vision for a company that would have a significant impact on health care, and that vision helped them hire top pros from across the sectors that touch the drug sector: insurers, pharmaceutical companies, PBMs, pharmacies, hospital systems, and technologists.

So Prescryptive wound up with a team that spoke a whole lot of different business languages, all trying to attack a complex problem that they all saw from different angles. Clearly articulating the company's purpose—the category it wanted to create—and getting everyone to orient around that same North Star was a challenge.

Chris admits that his team struggled to meet that challenge on their own. "And so we started researching and trying to figure out, where can we get some help?" Chris told us. "We were trying to differentiate ourselves, and we were trying to make it so that it could be understandable to folks who were in the market, but we didn't want to sound like everybody else. And the challenge with that is to differentiate but also meet people where they are. And that's a difficult challenge, particularly in a marketplace where not everybody understands how it works or what's broken."[2]

An advisor to the company suggested Chris should read *Play Bigger*. The concept and process the book describes resonated with Chris and Kevin, and they tried to use it to do category design themselves. But they struggled to run that play internally. That's when Chris reached out to us at CDA.

We told him we were confident we could help the company with an in-person, one-week workshop with his leadership team. We only found out later that Chris thought that was nuts. "I had a high degree of skepticism going in," he told us long after we worked together. "It's hard to imagine that you can spend a week on something that we'd been spending a lot more than a week trying to figure out and do ourselves, and had hired others to help us, to believe that you could actually get through it in a week and come out the other end with something that was substantial."

But actually, we find that the intensity of the compressed timeline is key to making a strategic category design project work.

In reality, we spend a lot more than a week on the whole process. Once we agree to work with a client, we spend a number of weeks on research. We dig in online and read all we can about the company. We also tell the company to identify the people who will participate in the workshop. We advise that the ideal number is from six to twelve, and they should have different leadership roles. The CEO and any cofounders must be there. The rest might be the product lead, the chief marketing officer, the head of sales, the chief financial officer, and so on. We insist that all of those chosen agree to be present in person for the full workshop. (In reality, we sometimes get someone joining via Zoom, but we discourage it.)

Once the participants are chosen, we send them each a questionnaire and follow those up with thirty-minute interviews. All that helps us understand the company's current position and where each participant will be coming from before we all meet. It also gets the participants thinking and talking about the questions we're asking, preparing them for our live session.

The workshop week is really four days. We tell the team to expect to all be in a room together for a full day on day one. The following two days, we do our work, which we'll explain in a moment. Then we're back together for a full day on day four. By the end of that fourth day, we expect that, together with the team, we will have agreed on a category for the company to create, and on a unifying category POV that captures the company's strategic direction.

Here's a brief glimpse of what happens over those four days.

Day one: Mike and Kevin (and anyone else CDA pulls into the project) lead a discussion about what problem the company really needs to solve, why the world needs this company to exist, why this company is the best one to solve the problem, and how the solution should work whether this or any company does it. We push the company to think bigger and funnel the conversation toward a conclusion, until everyone in the room gets pretty close to seeing the category and how to design it.

Days two and three: We do our work, which means we discuss on our own what we think came out of the first-day workshop, and then hammer out a POV that captures the category story in a narrative of about one thousand words. (There's much more on writing a POV in later chapters.) The POV needs to describe the problem, introduce the new category, describe the solution, and at the end show why the client company is the one to make the category come alive. The POV suggests a category name, and (especially relevant in the Prescryptive story) ends with a tagline for the company's brand.

Day four: We reassemble with everyone and present the POV to the room, showing it line by line on slides and reading it out loud. This sets a tone that finalizing the POV will be a group effort. The POV puts the outcomes of the first day's discussion right in front of the company's team to react to. Then the rest of the day is spent talking about the POV and, together, editing every word of it. At the end of that day, almost every time, the whole team buys into and aligns around the POV and the category strategy. They've all created it together. They all feel ownership.

Here's Chris's take on the process, from his CEO seat at Prescryptive: "The process in and of itself is educational for the team. It's like strategy. You get everybody on the leadership team into a room and you spend a week going through developing strategy. The value, as much as the deliverable that comes out the other end, is the actual process of driving the alignment conversation and getting everybody to understand, through a single lens. And so the process in and of itself is very aligning.

"And then I would say the last day is this epiphany type of experience where we still talk about it, years later," Chris said. "We still are anchored on the output from that meeting. Our tagline [that concluded the POV], 'Rewriting the script,' still has a massive effect on the company and the culture."

He added: "Going into the workshop, we framed the company in a completely different way than coming out of it."

We did the workshop with Prescryptive in January 2020. (Yes, it was in person, just before the pandemic shut the world down.) The impact on Chris's efforts to raise a round of funding was immediate. Chris told us, "A week or two after our workshop, I had a series of meetings at the J.P. Morgan Healthcare Conference—with twelve to fifteen brand-name venture funds. I went from hundreds of pitches and conversations where people knew the space but could not understand what we do—to, in less than ten minutes, they understood why we are different and understood what we do. That is success. So when we got to the right investor, it was easy and fast. We didn't get hung up on clarity. In fact, part of the benefit was getting to 'no' faster with some investors."

Those investor conversations led to Prescryptive's landing a $26 million A round. In the four years from then until we started writing this book, the category strategy and POV helped Prescryptive get traction in the market and hire great people. "It's because of our mission and the purpose that the company has. And people are leaving fifteen-year careers and industry-leading companies to join our purpose." The POV has helped Prescryptive talk effectively to customers and partners, Chris said. It's helped guide the marketing and branding.

By late 2024, Prescryptive's platform enabled health-care consumers to compare prices and payment options for prescriptions at more than sixty thousand pharmacies. It had forged an innovative partnership with another health-care tech company, Transcarent. "It's pretty amazing to see [the category work] come to fruition," Chris said.

Perception Versus Perspective

There are, no doubt, countless ways to practice strategic category design. Strategic category design isn't a franchise— like if you get a McDonald's franchise, you have to do everything the McDonald's way. It is instead a way of thinking and acting that leads to a strategy to win a new market category. Some companies, for instance, hire a resident category designer to drive category design through the organization on a daily basis, for years on end.

So why do we do it the way we do it, in a pressurized short burst?

For one, most companies don't have time (or money!) to waste. If it's possible to get to a category strategy in a few weeks, then why wouldn't you do it that way? Many big consulting firms might prefer to stretch out an engagement, throw a lot of people at it, do a lot of reports, and make it seem like the deliverable was a ton of work so the firm can charge a ton of money. We believe it's actually more valuable to the company if we streamline the process, go all out in a short burst, and get a high-quality result fast.

Second, we want to create intensity and momentum. Everyone is there to get something vital to the company done quickly. The top leaders set aside two full days (day one and day four, per above) just for the category design workshop. Some or all have traveled to be in the room in person. Those present feel special because they get to be in the room where it happens (to paraphrase *Hamilton*). The process pushes the team to work together. They bond. They end up feeling like they all played a part in the outcome, and so they buy into the outcome and become excited to evangelize the new POV and category to their internal teams and, then, to customers, partners, and other stakeholders. In the end, the workshop creates alignment among the team and ignites a sense of mission to go out and win the category.

Companies can do this on their own, and this book will show you how. Still, there are advantages to using outsiders (in general—not just us!) as a forcing function.

When you're inside a company, especially if you're a founder, one of the hardest things to do is to clearly see the company and product from the outside in—to see yourself as others see you. And yet if you can do that, it becomes a superpower.

You'll have an advantage over competitors, better know what products to build, and understand how to influence your target customers so they see you as you want them to see you.

One way to think about this is perception versus perspective. One popular TikTok video in 2024 was an interview with an unnamed ex-CIA agent explaining the concept and how perception versus perspective helps with spycraft. As he noted, perception is your interpretation of the world. Most of us rely only on our perception—after all, it's what's inside each of our brains, and it's hard to escape our own brains.

Yet as the spy guy said, there's no real advantage over others if you rely on your perception of things—because that's what everyone else does, too. And it's a disconnect from the reality that others experience.

Perspective, however, is the act of observing the world from outside yourself. Another way to put it, which we've heard a few times in the tech ecosystem, is to have radical empathy. It's a way to get out of your head and put yourself in the place of your target customers—to consider what they're worried about, what makes them happy, what motivates them, what they really need.

If you can do that, you can escape your perception that, for instance, your product is an amazing breakthrough that everyone should immediately rush to buy. You'll replace that thinking with a perspective on how others see your product. This leads to insights about, say, why your product isn't selling like crazy. If you can see that, you have an opportunity to change others' perceptions with highly effective messaging, or come to a realization that you need to tweak the product to truly meet the needs of your target market.

Sure, some say that perception *is* reality. In a way, that's true, because each person's perception is in fact their particular reality. But *your* perception is only *your* reality. It's not the reality of target customers. The challenge, then, is to get outside yourself and understand the reality of others.

Perception is essentially imaginary. It's a belief. It's not actually real. Which means that it can be altered because it's only neurons firing, not actual, physical, unalterable reality.

Uncovering the difference for a company between perception and perspective is one of the most valuable outcomes of strategic category design. The discipline of category design is centered on an outside-in approach to creating a new market category. The tools of category design are aimed at understanding the reality of target customers, empathizing with them, and getting deep into what they need and why they need it.

Perspective is also a reason outsiders bring value to the category design process. An outsider is not steeped in the company's perception of the world. They can see it from the outside in. (Some remarkable leaders can do that on their own, but not many.)

One way or another, a company's leaders need to break the spell of perception and clearly see the shift in context around the people they are targeting, what's now missing for them amid the current context, and what innovation would make their lives better.

Once a company gets its arms around that, it will see the new product category that needs to exist but doesn't—yet.

Strategic Category Design Outcomes

What about measurable outcomes of strategic category design?

Companies that implement it wind up with a much stronger message and position in the market, and alignment among the leadership team around a common North Star. Some get intangibles like a workforce morale boost and rejuvenated sense of purpose.

We've been doing this long enough to be certain that category design leads to positive outcomes. Since we mostly work with pre-IPO companies, we can't point to quarterly earnings or stock price trends. But we can see other indicators, like better-than-expected funding rounds, improved valuations, easier sales motions, and acquisitions.

For example, one client, Diligent, was valued at about $4 billion when we worked with the company in 2020. By 2024, it was valued at more than $7 billion. We can't claim that was all because of its category design initiative, but we're sure it helped. Another client, Hotel Engine (now known just as Engine), was valued at $500 million when it worked on category design with us; in September 2024, it raised a round at a $2.1 billion valuation.

About a year after we worked with LinkedIn Sales

Solutions (LSS) on developing its "deep sales" category, the division's VP of marketing at the time, Gail Moody-Byrd, wrote this on LinkedIn: "Since September, we've been filling rooms around the globe with customers and prospects like this who trust LinkedIn and value our advice and perspective on how to navigate uncertain times. With #deepsales, we've captured a moment where our offering matches the market's needs."

Some other outcomes, post–category design work:

- Tallarium was a London-based seed-stage startup when the company worked with us in the summer of 2021. In 2022, the company landed a series A round with a total of $8.7 million raised. Tallarium created a digital platform that helps traders in energy and other commodities discover "true value" pricing.
- Guidewheel was a seed-stage startup that worked with us in 2020, when it was still called Safi. Post–category design, it changed its name to Guidewheel and raised a series A round of $9 million. In the fall of 2024, it raised a B round of $31 million. From CEO Lauren Dunford: "Working with CDA to thoughtfully build the FactoryOps category laid the foundation for strong, aligned growth and product development." In 2024, Dunford was invited to be onstage at the World Economic Forum in Davos, Switzerland, and in 2025 was invited to deliver a main-stage TED Talk.

- The Predictive Index was, in 2019, sixty years old. It needed to reimagine itself, and category design helped it define the category of talent optimization. The company then raised $101 million in two rounds. From CEO Mike Zani: "The category work was instrumental in positioning us to raise a significant round of growth equity. It aligned the team in a way that was palpable. When operating a company and when pitching investors, that harmonic alignment is priceless."

Category design is not something that no one had ever thought to do. Throughout history, smart, innovative companies have created new market categories and designed them to their advantage. But those companies' leaders were doing it instinctively and ad hoc. When working out the discipline of category design, an important part was reverse engineering what others had successfully done by instinct, codifying it, and making it easy for anyone else to understand how to do it.

Any ambitious company should want to do everything it can to create and win a market category. One counterpoint we often hear is: "If it's a huge market category, there's room for lots of winners." Well, yeah, but that depends on how you define *winners*.

Most categories have a single clear winner. And that winner walks away with most of the economics—market share, profit share, valuation—of that category. The rest fight for relative scraps. But if that seems a little vague, at CDA we looked into a few specific and updated examples about some well-known category winners that have endured for years, if not decades.

We'll start with an old category that we first wrote about in *Play Bigger*: the minivan category. In 1983, Chrysler created the category when it introduced the first minivans, the Dodge Caravan and Plymouth Voyager. Chrysler did an amazing job of category design, selling us on the category of minivan, not just on its two branded models. The company established itself in people's minds as the category leader, and certainly won the dominant design—every competing minivan that has come after Chrysler's has looked pretty much like Chrysler's.

More than forty years later, this is the power of category dominance: In the US, Chrysler consistently maintains a 50 percent to 60 percent share of the minivan market, despite competition from Toyota, Honda, and others. Once a company embeds itself in our biases as the category leader, it's hard to unseat it, even if a competitor makes a product that is arguably better.

Google is another example of winning a category—internet search—and embedding itself in our biases. In reality, there is nothing that ever prevented any of us from using a different search engine. Google isn't like Facebook, LinkedIn, or Twitter, where you're glued there because your connections are there. Other search companies argue that they produce better results or do a better job protecting your privacy. The vast majority of us don't care. We just use Google.

So twenty-five years after Google was founded, its global

search market share stood at 92 percent. Second-place Bing scraped along at 3 percent. And what's the only threat to Google? The emergence of a *completely different* category of search (which is not really *search* anymore—it's more like *answer*) based on generative AI, such as ChatGPT or Perplexity.[3]

We learned from Salesforce's mission to create the then-new (in 1999, when the company was founded) market category of cloud CRM—at a time when most big companies dismissed cloud computing as too risky and untested. Salesforce's goal was to displace the old "on-premise CRM" category (big, expensive software that the buyer had to painfully maintain) with the new cloud CRM category (which let people use the software without installing or maintaining it). In a space crowded with hefty competitors such as Adobe, Microsoft, SAP, and HubSpot, Salesforce in 2024 held on to 31 percent of market share. While that's not at a Google level, it is a dominant position. The rest of the market is divided into tiny slivers among an enormous number of competitors.

Apple's iPhone is a fascinating example of category dominance. Certainly Apple established the dominant design of the smartphone category after it introduced the iPhone in 2007. Lots of different smartphone designs existed before that from the likes of BlackBerry, Handspring, Nokia, and Motorola. Since the iPhone solidified its position, there's really only been one design. Pretty much every competing phone made today looks and acts like the iPhone. Apple is the clear category winner. (Stay tuned—much more later about the iPhone and how it won the dominant design.)

Now the iPhone's absolute market share isn't that impressive. Samsung sells almost as many phones as Apple. Android phones in total sell more. But dig deeper, and all those other phone makers are barely making a profit. If you look at Apple's share of total smartphone profits, analysts at different times have figured that Apple takes in anywhere from 66 percent of the whole category's profits to a remarkable 103.6 percent! (In other words, everyone but Apple might have lost money.)[4] One typical advantage of category dominance is pricing power.

One more example: White Claw became the dominant design in the category of hard seltzer after its first product was introduced in 2016. The category didn't exist until then. In a flash, giant competitors such as AB InBev (maker of Budweiser) leapt into the category to take on the comparably tiny maker of White Claw, Mark Anthony Group. But it hardly mattered. White Claw in 2024 held on to about 45 percent of the US market in the category. Bud Light Seltzer had 10 percent.[5]

Not every company, of course, can be a category winner. The public usually wants every category to have competitors and choices. There are many, many good businesses built on being a distant second or third in someone else's category.

Yet as Chrysler, Apple, Salesforce, and others show, the path to outsize enduring success runs through category dominance. While there are no guaranteed ways to win a category, there are ways to improve a company's odds of winning a category—and that's what the process of strategic category design is all about.

2

Conditions for Strategic Category Design

Scott Kuper, a managing partner at the giant venture capital firm Andreessen Horowitz, in 2019 published *Secrets of Sand Hill Road: Venture Capital and How to Get It*—a straightforward, honest description of how VCs think. Here is perhaps the most revealing thing he wrote, and it says a lot about why a company would want to do all it can to define and win a market category:

> In VC, all we really care about is the at bats per home run. That is, the frequency with which the VC gets a

return of more than ten times her investment—which we consider a home run.

The fundamental assumption here is that ideas are not proprietary. In fact, VCs assume the opposite—if an idea turns out to be a good one, assume there will be many other founders and companies that are created to pursue this idea. So what matters most is, why do I as a VC want to back this particular team versus any of the x-number of other teams that might show up to execute this idea?

Thus, every investment decision has infinite opportunity cost in that it likely prevents you as a VC from investing in a direct competitor in that space; you have picked your horse to ride.

In light of this, among the cardinal sins of venture capital is getting the category right (meaning that you correctly anticipated that a big company could be built in a particular space) but getting the company wrong (meaning that you picked the wrong horse to back).[1]

OK, so let's parse that for how you, as a company leader, need to think if you want to chase outsize success.

VCs are looking for home runs, not singles or doubles. (The assumption here is that you, too, as company leader, want to hit a home run!) Most home runs are companies that define and win an important market category—companies like Salesforce, Airbnb, or Stripe. Singles and doubles are the copycats—the second- and third-place companies that win some market share but always operate in the shadow of the category winner—or companies that pursue a small category that won't matter much.

So your first layer of thinking should be about identifying a significant new market category with huge potential.

When you go to pitch investors, remember that they are first listening for whether this is a new market category that will be a home run. That's not the way founders usually approach a pitch. They go in trying to first sell the VC on the company itself.

But the VC really wants to be sold first on the category. To do that, you need to deeply understand the category and know how to articulate it.

Once an investor has an epiphany that this new category you're showing them is going to be huge, the investor's next layer of thinking is about whether your company is going to win it.

A smart founder will present a plan for doing that, and such a plan is what you get from a strategic category design process. You want to show how you are going to design the category in a way that favors your company and gives your company the best chance of winning it.

If you can't effectively tell that story, a smart VC who is excited about the category will dismiss you and then go looking for the company most likely to win the category. As Kuper pointed out, a cardinal sin of venture capital is to pick the right category and wrong company. Your job as a founder is to help the investor believe in *both* the category's potential *and* your company's ability to win the category.

Developing an engaging, category-forward pitch to raise

capital from the best investors is one of the top reasons companies implement category design.

A Cure for "Vision Entropy"

There are a handful of situations where category design can be a godsend. We'll detail the most common in this chapter. But we'll start with a story that will help illustrate one of those situations, which we call vision entropy.

In the late 1990s, the tech sector was abuzz about the exciting promise of a company called Teledesic. And then, in the early 2000s, Teledesic spun out of control until it flatlined. It was a classic case of vision entropy, which happens when a founder's or CEO's ambitions fall apart in disorganized pieces. It is a condition that frustrates many leaders who want to build something audacious that changes the way we live and work.

Here's how it played out with Teledesic:

The project was the brainchild of Craig McCaw, an entrepreneur who in the nineties built one of the nation's biggest cell phone networks. (It was later bought by AT&T.) McCaw started working on Teledesic in 1994, and then brought in Microsoft CEO Bill Gates. The two invested millions of their own money. Teledesic started out with some serious mojo.

The vision was huge. As the consumer internet exploded into our lives in the nineties, Teledesic planned to put into orbit 840 satellites that could provide a wireless digital connection to 95 percent of the planet. The satellites would hand off signals to one another in space by laser beams. Users would put a dinner plate–size satellite dish on a windowsill and get high-speed internet.

Of course, if you're reading this now, you're probably realizing this is basically Starlink, Elon Musk's highly successful satellite internet business. But back then, nothing like Teledesic had been tried, or maybe even conceived.

McCaw had the vision at a time when most people connected to the internet via dial-up modems. Cell networks could not yet carry data. Big swaths of the global population couldn't even make a phone call. McCaw believed he could make the internet available to everyone, everywhere.

Yet McCaw's vision alone wasn't enough. He ultimately failed to guide and manage all of the people and resources he needed to make Teledesic happen. Boeing and Motorola invested and joined the effort. A Saudi prince put in $200 million. Lockheed Martin got involved. All had agendas that veered from McCaw's. Before long, delays and design revisions angered contractors, who started to bail. The delays also gave time for land-based access to the internet to get much better, making Teledesic less necessary. In 2000, one analyst, Andrew Cole of Renaissance Strategy, told *USA Today*: "I bought into the dream many years ago, but the dream has passed its sell-by date." Teledesic shut down in 2002.[2]

Teledesic may be a dramatic illustration of vision entropy, but in the decades since, we've watched founders with big and not-so-big visions become frustrated by the same breakdown. The causes can be many, but a common thread is an inability to express and evangelize the vision so powerfully that everyone involved believes in the same goal and aligns around the strategy to get there.

Some founders struggle to express their vision in a way that others embrace and get excited about. Technical founders are often brilliant at conceiving and building a breakthrough product but aren't as good at converting the vision in their heads into language that guides and energizes the rest of the team and ecosystem. Everyone involved has their own interpretation of the vision, which in turn means they're likely to work toward different goals than the founder had in mind.

Sometimes founders start a business with just themselves or maybe one or two others. Then it's easy to verbally discuss the vision and constantly nudge a small team to keep them aligned. But once the company gets funding and some traction and the team grows in size, people come aboard who were not there at the beginning. They don't have the vision implanted in their brains from constant exposure to the founders. Some partners come in with different ideas or agendas. Before long, if you assembled all the key players in a room and asked each to verbalize the vision, they'd all say something different.

Once that kind of entropy starts, it's hard to reverse. And that's what happened to McCaw.

There are ways to battle vision entropy. Writing out a straightforward, crisp narrative of the vision—a POV—is a powerful way to implant the vision in the existing team and indoctrinate newcomers. And the process of getting to the written-down vision can be as important as the finished document.

To do that process well—as noted earlier—debate and develop the POV along with key members of the leadership team. By going through the exercise together, everyone gets excited about the shared vision because they feel they helped shape it. They're less likely to second-guess the strategy the minute something goes a bit wrong or veer from the strategy to appease some customer or investor. When each member of the core team goes back to their various teams, they all evangelize the same message.

The process itself pushes the leadership team to make hard decisions about the details of the vision and how to get there. These are decisions about who the company is and how it wants to be seen by the outside world.

The POV becomes like the musical score for an orchestra. Everyone plays the same symphony, even though each has only a small role in creating the whole. The main job of the conductor (i.e., the CEO) is to set and maintain the tempo and make sure the pieces are coming together as a whole.

If McCaw and Gates had created and socialized a strong POV for Teledesic, they might have stood a better chance of keeping all the partners in line, meeting deadlines, and moving forward. And while Musk built Starlink at a different time with better and cheaper technology (and the advantage of owning a rocket company that could put satellites into orbit), he had long been good at writing out a vision and strategy and evangelizing it.

Founders who feel like they are battling vision entropy can find help in the strategic category design process.

Seven Additional Common Syndromes

Vision entropy is just one syndrome that category design can help alleviate.

When we work with company leadership teams, sometimes we're like personal trainers—the company is in good shape and knows what it wants to accomplish, and so its leaders use strategic category design to get the company in the best condition possible to win its market category. These are companies that could have been doubles or triples on their own, and category design helps boost them to a home run.

But other times, a company has an issue, some discomfort, chronic pain, and first needs a diagnosis. We've seen a handful of common conditions that strategic category design can address. Here are seven more of those conditions. Some companies experience more than one of these at once.[3]

Build-It-and-They-Will-Come Syndrome: Cool Product but Tepid Demand

Some companies, often those started by technical founders, build an amazing product—and are so proud of the product that they understandably want to tell the world everything about it. But these founders may have a hard time telling potential customers in plain language why anyone *needs* such a product.

In fact, if you look at the vast majority of technology company websites, the first thing you see is some big typeface that announces what the product is, what it does, and some technical detail about speed or power or whatever—all of which makes potential customers have to figure out what that product is good for. What those customers want to know is what problem you'll solve for them!

How do you know if your company suffers from build-it-and-they-will-come syndrome? Look for common symptoms such as: Sales can't get past early adopters; investors wonder about product-market fit; marketing overemphasizes features and struggles to get buyers interested in the core idea; analysts put it in the wrong category; and investor decks leave VCs underwhelmed because they don't see a problem worth investing in.

To fix this, the company leaders need to set aside their desire to talk about the product and instead go deep on what problem the company wants to solve. Once a company can precisely describe the problem, potential customers can better understand why the product is valuable, moving them closer to buying.

Outcomes include clearer communication with potential investors, customers, employees, and partners; easier fundraising; a more convincing sales story to tell; insight into who to *stop* selling to; and analyst clarity about the company's category.

Spinning Strategic Compass: Many Possible Directions; Not Enough Agreement

Startups usually begin with one product, one mission, and a clear goal. As companies scale, hire new leaders, make acquisitions, and start new product lines, the mission and goals can grow branches. Leadership team members may have different ideas about where the company should go next. Often, various team members give too much weight to what they're hearing from customers—understandable, because pleasing the best customers is good for the bottom line. But customers are usually looking for tweaks that benefit them in the short run. They aren't going to have a vision for a category-defining product that takes a giant leap forward and gives them something they've never seen before.

One of our clients, London-based Zedsen, came to us because it had a technological breakthrough called electrical capacitance tomography, which could've had dozens of different applications that ranged from health care to airport security. The company kept chasing a wide range of opportunities with its limited resources, and it wasn't getting serious traction anywhere. Through the category design process, the team was able to focus on one problem to solve and one product to build: a handheld device that could noninvasively detect breast cancer. The strategy then focused on gaining momentum for that product before moving to adjacent markets.

Common symptoms of spinning strategic compass include: unaligned leadership team; confusion in the ranks about strategy; mixed messages to the public; no clear "flag on the hill" to charge toward; and strategic initiatives that are constantly reexamined, underinvested in, or perpetually put on hold.

To help fix this condition, the leadership team can go through the category design process to develop one strategic POV that everyone on the team buys into. The company has a new story to be guided by—a clear flag on the hill that every part of the company can march toward.

Outcomes include: alignment at the top; clear message to employees about the company mission; clear communication to and increased credibility with the marketplace and investors; confidence in decisions to invest in or shut down product lines or business units, or to make acquisitions or enter into strategic partnerships.

Category Jail: Stuck in a Crowded Space; Can't Get Out

When buyers and analysts don't understand why a company's offering is different, they stick that company in an existing, familiar market category, which can mean it gets grouped in with dozens or even hundreds of other companies. Investors see the company as a copycat. Potential customers barely see it at all among all the noise.

In 2021, we got a call from Ragy Thomas, CEO of New York–based Sprinklr. The company was preparing for an IPO. Analysts and a lot of potential customers and investors thought of Sprinklr as another company in a crowded customer experience management, or CXM, category. But Ragy believed Sprinklr was doing something different and was miscategorized. If Sprinklr was going to go public, Ragy wanted the company to stand out and be valued as a category creator instead of a category follower.

As we took the Sprinklr team through the category design process, they realized that while other CXM companies were offering software to help with individual aspects of a customer's experience, Sprinklr's system pulled all of those together for a universal view of every aspect of a customer's experience. The company was creating a category of unified customer experience management, or UCXM. When the company wrote its S1—the document that describes the company for investors—it built its story around the UCXM category. There is no way to know how much the category positioning added to the IPO price, but Ragy was confident it was significant. Investors like a clearly articulated unique story—especially when it describes a new market category.

Most company leaders are aware if they've been put in category jail. Symptoms include investor indifference; ineffective marketing messages that rely on arguing on specs like faster, cheaper, and bigger; analysts always placing the company in a crowded category; potential customers evaluating the product with the wrong criteria; and too few inbound sales.

The first step toward getting out of category jail is uncovering what unique problem the company needs to aim at—one it can define and solve. The key to category design is understanding and expressing why the company or product is different. The goal is to move the company into a favorable position in its own unique category.

Outcomes include clear differentiation; analysts moving the company to an appropriate emerging category; a faster and easier sales cycle; and fundraising on more favorable terms.

Chronic Fatigue Syndrome: In Need of Reenergizing

Some companies that have been successful for a long time—ten, twenty, even sixty years—need a next act. There's nothing terribly wrong, but the sense of mission has frayed and forward drive seems stuck in low gear.

We've seen this up close a few times. Earlier we mentioned The Predictive Index, based in the Boston area. The company was sixty years old when CEO Mike Zani and his partners bought it. And for decades, it had been a leader in developing tests that could help businesses make hiring decisions. Yet the tests alone would no longer be enough to stay competitive in an increasingly crowded field. If the company didn't renew itself, it likely would have lost its relevance.

However, all those decades of testing meant that The Predictive Index had decades of anonymized data about people's skills and strengths and weaknesses. Zani and his team realized the company could use that data to inform software based on the science of teams, and create something that would give the company a whole new North Star. As his leadership group worked through strategic category design, they landed on the category of talent optimization—a new, data-driven way to help people within an organization know how to best work with one another and form teams of complementary strengths. The new category helped reenergize the company. As of this writing, The Predictive Index pitches itself as "the only science-backed platform that gives HR leaders and people managers the insight to get hiring, management, and engagement right—before problems start."

For most older companies, common symptoms of chronic fatigue syndrome include slowing growth; a sense that competitors are catching up or bypassing it; a product that only incrementally improves; fear that the company is losing its place in the zeitgeist.

Category design takes a company through a discussion of the "adjacent possible." (Much more on that later.) Exciting new products and services are born in the adjacent possible. Many fatigued companies are stuck in what was possible yesterday. Category design helps the company find a new version of itself that pushes its mission out to the adjacent possible.

Outcomes can include a renewed purpose; a compelling narrative; de-positioning of competitors; resurrected growth; improved morale; and revenue acceleration.

Impractical Futurism: Too Far Ahead with a Big Idea

Many brilliant founders can so clearly see the future, they believe it's already here. They build a product that's directionally right, yet the technology doesn't quite work well enough and potential customers don't yet grasp why they'd want it. While these companies can get funded, the big risk is running out of money before the future happens.

In the 2020s, a company called Humane was a high-profile case. It developed an AI-driven pin that could supposedly take the place of a smartphone, and raised more than $230 million from high-profile investors. But while the vision was enticing and might have been an early view of the future of personal communications, the technology necessary to make it work wasn't ready. Reviewers trashed the pin. (Headline in *Engadget*, April 2024: "The Humane AI Pin Is the Solution to None of Technology's Problems.")[4] In February 2025, the company's assets were bought by HP Inc. for $116 million and the entire operation was shut down. The pins ceased to work and became useless to anyone who owned one.

How can a company recognize if it's too far ahead of

technology and society? Well, it finds that the product is very difficult to build, and it seems like science fiction to much of the public. The company can't sell beyond early adopters; it has a high burn rate; and while it may get fawning media at first, that attention doesn't translate into revenue.

This is another application of the adjacent possible. If the company is too far ahead of what's possible, the conversation needs to turn toward how to create a product today that lands in the adjacent possible. Then the leadership team needs to articulate a plan for developing the product over time and pulling potential customers from what they know today to the future the company wants to create.

Outcomes include a clear product road map; easier sales; company-sustaining revenue; bigger subsequent rounds of funding; and a broader understanding of how we move from where we are today to where the company wants to take us.

No Time to Lose: Need a Boost to Win a Heated Race

Some companies find themselves in a category that promises to become huge, but there's still no clear category winner among many contenders. The company needs a competitive advantage to increase its odds of winning the category while de-positioning contenders. It's like the old cartoon character Popeye, who needed to down a can of spinach to get a boost to win a fight.

These situations can often feel electric. The company

can sense the category and the stakes. We felt that when we worked with LinkedIn's Sales Solutions division, a billion-dollar business unit that offers a version of LinkedIn to sales people to help them find and address potential customers. The product had been around for a decade, but competitors were coming at it from all directions. The sales profession was changing because of technology and societal shifts. Somebody was going to understand this change and create a new category of product for sales professionals. LinkedIn wanted to define and win that category. Through category design, the Sales Solutions team came to understand that selling now means deeply knowing and connecting with potential customers, and no company was better positioned to create a product that could do that. The team landed on the category deep sales, rebuilt its product around the category concept, and went to market with a new category that depositioned its competitors.

Common symptoms of having no time to lose include an internal sense of alarm about winning the category; paranoia about competitors; potential customers waiting for a clear winner before buying; and VCs continuing to fund contenders. Category design can help conceptualize the category, write its story, and set the category rules in a way that gives the company a better chance to win the category over time.

Outcomes include increased visibility of the company; competitors falling away; inbound demand; analysts identifying the company as the category leader; less competition for customers; and more outright wins.

Fundraising-Story Anemia: About to Seek Funding or IPO but Need a Stronger Narrative

As discussed at the start of this chapter, a clear story that describes creating and winning a differentiated category can make the difference between a so-so round of fundraising and a great one. We've run into many companies that know what category they're building yet have difficulty putting together a powerful investor deck or S1 that tells that story.

Sprinklr was stuck in category jail, but that overlapped with its need to tell a stronger story for its IPO. Countless companies have used the category design process to find the right story to tell in investor pitch decks. As noted earlier, Guidewheel in 2020 worked with us to find its story, which helped it build a deck that led to a series A round of $9 million and then a B round of $31 million, while also getting the company on the radar of the World Economic Forum and TED.

Common symptoms of story anemia are an investor deck or S1 that doesn't seem differentiated; potential investors needing to ask a lot of questions before understanding the business case; investment bankers or VCs giving a valuation lower than the company believes is right; and valuations based solely on past history and not on the future vision.

A category POV gives the company a story to tell that is logical and easy to understand, and differentiates the company for investors who want to put their money into a category-defining company.

Outcomes can include better valuations; investors quickly grasping why they want to invest; and investors feeling they're buying into an important category of product or service, not just the company.

But Don't Get the Whole Category Wrong

Investors want to get excited about a category they believe will be enormous, and invest in the company that will win it. Their nightmare is getting the category right and the company wrong.

But then there's a flip side: a fascinating company that gets the category all wrong. You don't want to put your money into that company. It's an extreme version of build-it-and-they-will-come syndrome.

General Magic is a legendary example. Founded in 1990, it essentially tried to build the entire consumer internet way too early. It got a lot of the concepts about the web and mobile devices right, but too early to make the technology work or convince the public it was worthwhile. The product was cool but didn't solve anyone's real problem—it was really just a toy. Yet Motorola, Sony, AT&T, Goldman Sachs, and Japan's telecom giant NTT all invested or signed on as partners. Apple took a minority stake and then-CEO John Sculley joined the board. But, similar to Teledesic, the category didn't emerge in time and the actual internet bypassed it. By 1999 General Magic was collapsing, and it shut down in 2004.

Segway was the same kind of story. Founded in 2001, John Doerr, then one of the hottest VCs in Silicon Valley, and Amazon's Jeff Bezos both invested. Apple CEO Steve Jobs predicted the Segway scooters would revolutionize cities. Founder and CEO Dean Kamen was quoted saying the Segway "will be to the car what the car was to the horse and buggy," and Doerr predicted the Segway would be "bigger than the internet."[5]

The original Segway was a technological marvel that wowed the public. But it utterly failed to create a meaningful category. Few people felt they needed one. Even now, the main problem it seems to solve is to help tourists who don't want to walk to see the sights. In 2015, Segway was bought by a Chinese company, which shut down production of the Segway "personal transporter" in 2020.

A category design exercise can help a company gain an outside perspective of itself, which can help it see whether the category it is creating is actually viable.

What the Knuckleball Can Tell Us About Categories Gone Wrong

Since VCs use the baseball metaphor of home runs, here's a surprising story of what happens when someone offers a great product in an inconsequential category. It's about the fate of the knuckleball in Major League Baseball.[6]

The lack of a robust market category for the knuckleball is why, in 2024, the MLB had one player—Matt Waldron of the

San Diego Padres—throwing the knuckleball, even though a good knuckleball pitcher can be immensely effective.

Back in the late 1990s, when your coauthor Kevin was a journalist at *USA Today*, he traveled to Oakland to spend some time with Tom Candiotti, then a knuckleball-throwing starting pitcher for the Oakland A's. At the time, there were three other knuckleball pitchers in the majors (Tim Wakefield, Red Sox; Steve Sparks, Angels; and Dennis Springer, Rays). A knuckler is the slowest pitch in baseball. It clocks in at between 40 mph and 65 mph, in a game that values pitchers who fire fastballs that top 95 mph. The knuckleball, as baseball fans know, doesn't spin and wobbles unpredictably on its way to the plate, which is both its blessing (batters don't know where it's going) and its curse (the pitcher and catcher don't know where it's going, either).

One moment in the Oakland game captured a lot about the knuckleball. Candiotti was on the mound. Joe Randa of the Detroit Tigers was at bat. Candiotti wound up and tossed a knuckleball toward the plate. As Kevin wrote in his story, "It veers at the last second on the batter. Randa turns and the pitch hits him dead-on in the back. Randa doesn't flinch. He trots to first, acting more like he's been hit with a shuttlecock than a pitched baseball. The umpire pulls out a new ball and throws it to Candiotti—faster than the pitch that had come in."

Still, in its own way, the knuckleball has been a killer product. The knuckleball was invented, baseball scholars say, by a pitcher named Toad Ramsey in the 1880s. In all the time since, the pitch has been mastered by only about two dozen major leaguers. But, astonishingly, three of them (Phil Niekro, Hoyt Wilhelm, and Pop Haines) are in the Hall of Fame. So about 12.5 percent of all knuckleball pitchers became Hall of Famers. Think about what that says about the effectiveness of the knuckleball. There have been about 20,500 players in major league history. If 12.5 percent of them made the Hall, there would be 2,562 Hall of Fame players. You know how many players are in the Hall? 270. A little more than 1 percent.

Knuckleball pitchers come with other attributes managers and front-office types should value—like, they can pitch more often because the knuckleball is easy on the arm, and they can pitch until they're old by pro sports standards. Candiotti was forty when Kevin interviewed him.

Why, then, does the game have just one knuckleballer today? It comes down to market perception. The market has been conditioned to dismiss the knuckleballer in favor of flame-throwing fastballers. As Kevin explained it in the story: "Most baseball people seem to think the knuckleball's disadvantages outweigh the advantages, so there's a negative spiral at work. The major leagues send the message that they only want hard throwers, so only kids who throw hard tend to become pitchers. No prospect is going to waste time practicing the knuckleball, so it becomes more scarce. Fewer coaches get comfortable with it, so the anti-knuckleball message gets stronger."

If you look at that through a category design lens, it sounds like some of the companies build a really cool product, and then hardly anyone knows what to do with it, like the Segway.

And if that's true, the situation for knuckleballers isn't going to change even if another truly great knuckleballer comes along. The only way to change this would be to condition the market—in this case, the market is baseball coaches, scouts, and executives—so it believes it needs knuckleballers.

That's where the *design* part of strategic category design can help. If you're running a company, maybe you recognize that you're building a knuckleball—a really good product that just doesn't have market acceptance. It has no category. Investors don't believe in the category. And it won't have a category unless your company designs and nurtures it, conditioning the market to believe it needs what you offer.

3

Market/Product Fit

If the goal is to create and win a market category, then it's helpful to establish what we mean by a market category.

It's actually a space in people's brains. So for a company leader, creating a new market category means opening up a new space in your potential customers' brains.

In 2024, *The New York Times* published a story about how electric vehicles were finally going fully mainstream. In the story, Randy Parker, CEO of Hyundai Motor America, which was about to start making electric cars in the state of Georgia, said: "The E.V. market has hit an inflection point. The early adopters have come. They've got their cars. Now you're starting to see us transition to a mass market."[1]

As little as five years before that, when most people thought about buying a new car, they rarely considered whether to buy an electric car. They just considered which gas-powered car to buy. The category of electric car did not really have a place in most people's minds. Consumers likely knew about electric cars, but more as a curiosity, not a practicality.

You can see that in the market share numbers. In 2020, the share of new cars purchased that were electric was 2 percent. In years prior to that, it was near zero. In 2023, the share of new cars purchased that were electric jumped to 10 percent, and it's been rising fast. This tells us that there is now a viable space in many people's minds for the category of electric cars. How did that happen?

Electric cars have been around for almost the entire history of automobiles. From time to time, a major automaker would put out an electric model that would ultimately flop. The category of electric car was something rabid environmentalists considered a real category, but for everyone else, it was an oddity. The range of those early electric cars sucked. Most of them looked geeky. (Anybody remember General Motors' EV1? It was introduced in 1996 and looked like it came out of Woody Allen's movie *Sleeper*. Only 1,200 were sold.)[2]

Tesla changed that starting in 2008, when it introduced its Roadster, which quickly created a new category we might call desirable electric car. It's hard to say how much of Tesla's category creation strategy was intentional, but starting with the Roadster was brilliant. That model was supercool and rocketfast. Car reviewers slobbered over it. A Roadster's price tag started at $109,000, and wealthy people lined up to buy.

The Roadster planted the seed of a desirable electric car category. Yet that wasn't enough to create a new space in the public's minds that said electric cars are a good alternative to gas cars. Over the next decade, Tesla continued to define the new category. It built more affordable sedans. It built out charging stations. We all started seeing more Teslas on the streets. The headspace to consider electric cars became more real.

But category creation magic only really happens when a new space becomes bigger than its creator—bigger than one brand. That got real around 2017, when General Motors made a radical announcement that it was aiming to make its entire fleet electric by 2035. (No, not EV1 successors. GM learned its lesson.) Ford, Hyundai, Mercedes-Benz, and others announced that they, too, would make mainstream electric vehicles. Newcomers like Rivian dove into the space.

All those competitors helped validate what Tesla started. An ecosystem was developing to support the category. The Hyundai executive recognized in 2024 that the category of electric cars—viable, practical electric cars—had been implanted in many buyers' brains as a worthy alternative to gas cars.

And once the category was established, Tesla and all its competitors had a market to sell into. Without that space in people's minds, there would be no market.

What does this tell you if you are launching a product or service that you believe creates a new market category?

It is as important to open up the category space in your audience's minds as it is to market your brand and features. In category design, we call this conditioning the market. If the space in people's brains doesn't exist, your offering has no place to go. Your audience doesn't understand how it fits into their lives. All of your marketing will be like throwing a ball at a brick wall. It won't penetrate.

Think of the category as bigger than your company. The category should be something that must exist, whether you participate in it or not. You should hope competitors come into the category. That validates and strengthens the category, helping establish the space in people's minds. If competitors don't come in, you may be trying to create a category that doesn't matter that much. (Segway!) If it mattered, others would see it, too.

While you want the category to be bigger than your company, you also want to set the rules and expectations for the category so others have to follow them. As Tesla opened up the desirable electric car category, its design led the way—from the fact that the cars look as stylish as gas-powered counterparts to the screens inside and the way charging works. Now GM and other automakers have to mimic those design choices because consumers expect them in an electric car. That, in turn, puts Tesla in the driver's seat (so to speak) of the category.

Ultimately, your goal is to develop the category and at the same time persuade your target customers to think of your brand first. You want to foster the belief that you are the leader driving the category's advancement. The company that achieves this typically holds on to the greatest market share of the category.

Why "Product/Market Fit" Is Backward

In June 2007, Marc Andreessen wrote a blog post titled "The Only Thing That Matters." It was the first use of the term *product/market fit*—which, Andreessen declared, is the only thing that matters.[3]

These days, product/market fit is a term you hear constantly in the tech startup ecosystem. Every company is looking for product/market fit.

Except they really should be looking for market/product fit.

That may seem like a nuance, but it's not. Product/market fit implies that you build a product and then find a market that demands it. But strategic category design suggests a different approach. Startups can gain traction sooner by identifying and creating a market first, then building the product that the market needs. In other words, market/product fit.

Marc's article isn't wrong—in fact, it's fantastically right in many ways, and perfectly describes why category design is such a powerful strategic discipline. He starts out by noting that there are three key elements to a startup: team, product, and market. He goes on to break down the relative importance of each to a startup's success.

A lot of VCs will say that the team is the key element—that a great team will figure out how to build a great product that addresses a great market. But it's not unheard-of for a great team to build a great product that can't find a market. In the late 1990s, Dean Kamen put together a brilliant team to build breakthrough technology, and they came out with the Segway. The Segway showed that a great team or product doesn't necessarily create a market.

Marc's article points out another scenario from the late 1990s that involved personal computer operating systems—a market segment then totally dominated by Microsoft's Windows. "Here's the classic scenario: the world's best software application for an operating system nobody runs. Just ask any software developer targeting the market for BeOS, Amiga, OS/2, or NeXT applications what the difference is between a great product and a big market." (If you weren't around in the 1990s, those were all PC operating systems that tried to compete with Windows but failed to make a dent, and have long since disappeared.)

So Marc deduces that the single most important factor in a startup's success isn't team or product—it's the market. When a big and hungry market spots a product it needs, the market literally sucks the product out of the company that makes it. "The product doesn't need to be great; it just has to basically work. And, the market doesn't care how good the team is, as long as the team can produce that viable product," Marc wrote. "In short, customers are knocking down your door to get the product; the main goal is to actually answer the phone and respond to all the emails from people who want to buy."

But here's where Marc stopped short: He didn't suggest that there's anything a company's leaders can do about the market. His article implies that the market is either there or not there and that a company's main job should be to build a product that will be demanded by a significant market. Hence "product/market fit"—either you build a product and search for a market that demands it, or you see a big market and build a product to satisfy it.

But market/product fit is a more proactive way of thinking about that. If the market is the single most important factor in a startup's success, then why wouldn't a startup begin by developing a market—and designing it so it favors that company?

Markets don't just exist or appear out of thin air. Someone creates them. They are, as we pointed out with Tesla, a space in people's minds. Tesla created that space for electric cars. Similarly, Apple created a market for tablets—something almost no one wanted before the iPad. White Claw created a market for hard seltzer. Now there are whole supermarket shelves for hard seltzer. Those weren't there a decade ago.

Since a market is a space in people's minds, then if a company builds a product for a space that doesn't exist, the product won't sell. A great product might open a space and create a great market on its own, but it also might not—so why leave it to chance?

The intent of category design is to engineer a new market. The process starts with identifying an important "missing"—something the world needs, even if the world doesn't yet know it needs that something. There might not yet be a space in people's minds for such a missing, but it's possible to create that space through education, messaging, advertising, and PR. Doing so requires clearly articulating the space so that target customers can see it—and demand a product that addresses it.

In short, the course of action is: Identify the market category; design the category; and market the category. A company that thinks this way can develop a market that will demand its product.

By thinking like this, something else magical happens. When a company so clearly understands a new space, it deeply understands what product to build to satisfy that space. It's an outside-in strategy—see and build the market, then build the product.

Again, Marc was absolutely right about the market being the key to everything. But the most savvy company leaders won't leave the market to chance. They'll build their own.

Once a company leadership team gets into the market/product fit mindset, they can build on that with what we call category-led growth. This, again, is a twist on conventional thinking about product-led growth. Creating a category that demands a product works better than creating a product that hopefully generates demand.

Bill Macaitis, who was the chief marketer at Slack, talked about the need to start with the category and work back to product and demand. "You see so many great tools coming out right now," he told us during an interview on the *Category Thinkers* podcast in 2024. "The ones that succeed are the ones that are rooted in pain." He went on to explain how the category strategy is the launch pad for a solid go-to-market strategy. "You have to have that solid foundation, you have to have really thought about what the category is, what it looks like. What are the pain points that you're solving? You have to have the category-led approach."[4]

Done well, category-led growth is a force multiplier for all of a company's other efforts. Then, when you build a great product and fire up a clever marketing campaign, the strength of the category's pull makes those efforts more fruitful.

What Monster Trucks Can Tell Us about Developing a Strong Category

Maybe you've heard of an event called Monster Jam. Monster truck shows are a big business these days. In the 1980s, Kevin met with the guy who created the monster truck category, Bob Chandler. Looking back, Chandler's story makes for an interesting case study in creating a new space in people's minds, fostering a category, and taking advantage of category-led growth.[5]

In a town outside St. Louis, Chandler built what is recognized as the first monster truck, which he named Bigfoot. The monster truck phenomenon was an accident, and at the time he didn't quite understand its appeal.

Here's the backstory: In 1974, Chandler was a construction worker who bought a Ford F-250 four-wheel-drive pickup truck. He got into off-roading in his truck and figured others would like to do that, too. But there weren't any shops in town catering to that pastime. So he opened one, Midwest Four Wheel Drive and Performance Center.

Chandler and his mechanics liked tinkering, so they kept putting bigger tires on the F-250 and adding steering systems and axles that would let the truck drive over bigger things. Eventually they found tires that were ten feet high and put them on the truck.

Here's what Chandler said happened next: "We put a couple of cars in a farmer's field and went out to see if it would work driving over them. We videotaped it, showed it back at the shop, and they cracked up. A promoter saw it and wanted to do it in front of people. I wondered. It seemed so destructive. We had a good rapport with the kids, and I didn't want to ruin it. But the crowd loved it. They went wild."

Nearly four decades later, we've realized that Chandler didn't just build one truck—he created a market category called monster trucks. As word of Bigfoot got around, others wanted to build similar trucks. They'd call Chandler to get some insight. "So I told them how I did it," he told me in 1985. "I'm just like that. But I don't know if it was too smart."

Actually, it was really smart. Helping form a market category legitimized Bigfoot, opened a space in people's minds that monster trucks were a new kind of fun, and generated category-led growth. The act of monster trucks driving over cars became more than an oddity—it turned into an accepted form of entertainment. If Chandler had held tight to his secrets, there may not be Monster Jams or so many other monster truck shows filling big-city arenas today. Bigfoot might have been an orphan.

Bigfoot 4X4 is now a huge business. It does shows all over the world—even the O2 Arena in London. It has a team of twelve drivers, including Chandler, now in his eighties, and sells clothing, toys, posters, and coffee mugs. Creating a far bigger pie benefited Chandler and Bigfoot. And the truck even made an appearance in the Burt Reynolds movie *Cannonball Run II*.

By the way, when Kevin showed up to interview Chandler in the eighties, Chandler thought Kevin should experience a show. Kevin didn't realize that Chandler meant he should experience one from *inside* the truck. Chandler drove, of course, while Kevin was white-knuckling it in the passenger seat.

Here's what Kevin wrote in his story:

"Here he comes," wails an announcer, "the original mon-nnnster trrrruck, Biiiiigfoooooot!" The star takes its cue, roars to life and rips into three junk cars bunched under the spotlight. The front end of the 14,000-pound Ford truck pops into the air, wheels momentarily spinning free. The modified monster then slams down on one rooftop. Glass shatters, the car's roof collapses, and Bigfoot bounces over all three cars, turns around and heads back for more.

This time the driver gets more height and the truck pounds down like a wrecking ball. The arm-thick treads chew up the cars as Bigfoot powers across the pile of junk and rolls to a halt. The driver opens the door and waves to a cheering, rollicking crowd.

Yes, Kevin was in the cab for all of that, witnessing market/product fit at close range.

4

The Category Creation Formula

As we worked with companies on category design for a decade, we learned more and more about market categories, why they exist, and how category designers see new opportunities. Eventually, we realized there is a category creation formula. Once we put it to use, we discovered that it is a simple and powerful generator of creative thinking about category design.

This is the formula:

$$f(\text{category}) = \text{context} + \text{missing} + \text{innovation}$$

And here's what all that means:

Context is what's changing or has changed for the audience you (the company) want to address. And we mean the whole context. Advances in technology such as AI are an important part of a context shift. New technology can open up new ways to solve old unsolvable problems. Technology can also create new problems that didn't exist before and now need to be solved. But context can also include economic conditions, changes in societal norms, or geopolitical upheaval. It might include wars or pandemics that, for instance, disrupt supply chains or cut off markets.

Context is the place to start a strategic category design discussion. Yet in our experience it is almost never where a company leadership team starts a strategic discussion. Thoroughly understanding the context around your audience is key to discovering a new category to create. Get your team together, set aside your marketing messages and product development road maps, and instead spend a chunk of time diving deep into the changes swirling around your potential customers.

The greater the changes in context, the more opportunities open up for creating new market categories. The 2020s have brought on, for better or worse, the most significant context shift in generations. The arrival of powerful AI alone is an enormous technological context shift. The 2020 COVID pandemic profoundly changed our relationship to work and workplaces. Geopolitical realignments are roiling markets, economies, and supply chains.

Missing is what will become evident from the context discussion. This is the magic of the formula. If you thoroughly understand the context, then you start to see what's missing—something that does not yet exist but that could solve a new problem that the context has created, or solve an old problem in a way the new context makes possible. You will realize the world is desperately missing this solution, and people will need it whether your company builds it or not. Once that missing thing comes into focus for your team, it will inevitably lead you to . . .

Innovation, which is the product or service that must be invented to address what's missing. This is where your team's unique expertise comes into play. What is the innovation you could build? How will it work? How will it solve for the missing in a way nothing else does?

Once you put those elements together, your team will see a category waiting—needing!—to be created.

The category creation formula leads to the most impactful categories of products and services because it surfaces a product or service the world needs. Such products or services are must-haves, not just nice-to-haves. The category creation formula is an outside-in, market-driven way of landing on a strategy. It helps you first see the category to create, then understand the product to build to win that category.

If you don't do any other part of strategic category design with your team, just take this formula and work it through together. In our workshops, we sometimes write the words *context, missing,* and *innovation* atop three columns on a whiteboard, and then fill in the columns as observations surface in the discussion. We've heard of some companies putting the formula up on a conference room wall so it informs every product and strategy conversation. However you do it, keeping the formula top of mind will do wonders for how you develop your product, motivate your team, and tell your story.

Great category designers seem to instinctively use the formula. One of the most admired category designers of all time is Apple's Steve Jobs. If you look back at his introduction of the iPhone in 2007, his presentation followed the category creation formula.[1]

"So, before we get into it, let me talk about a category of things," Jobs said at the unveiling, right away setting us up to think about new categories of products.

Then Jobs warmed us up by first setting the context and then pointing out what was missing. He continued: "The most advanced phones are called smart phones, so they say. And they typically combine a phone plus some email capability, plus they say it's the Internet. It's sort of the baby Internet into one device, and they all have these little plastic keyboards on them. And the problem is that they're not so smart and they're not so easy to use, and so if you kind of make a Business School 101 graph of the smart axis and the easy-to-use axis, phones, regular cell phones are right there, they're not so smart, and they're not so easy to use."

That's all context, bleeding into some of what's missing. Then Jobs landed a solid punch about what's missing: "What we want to do is make a leapfrog product that is way smarter than any mobile device has ever been and is super-easy to use."

After that, Jobs told us about the innovation: "So, we're going to reinvent the phone. Now, we're going to start with a revolutionary user interface. It is the result of years of research and development, and of course, it's an interplay of hardware and software."

All of that came before he ever showed an iPhone, mentioned the iPhone brand, or ran through the iPhone's features. (Isn't that backward from just about every new product introduction you've ever seen?) First, Jobs wanted to make us see the need for something like the iPhone. Keep in mind that up to that point, most of us were pretty enamored with the day's smartphones. Businesspeople loved their BlackBerrys. Devices like the Treo were winning over consumers. Jobs helped us see something we didn't see before— that all those devices were part of the problem. What was missing was a device that would be easy to use, powerful, have a big screen, and allow for apps that could make the phone do almost anything.

Steve Jobs's iPhone introduction followed the formula: He teed up the context, made us see the missing, and then told us about the innovation—all before unveiling the product.

Now, interestingly, compare that to how current Apple CEO Tim Cook introduced the company's $3,500 Vision Pro mixed-reality goggles in 2023. Cook didn't use the formula. He didn't employ market/product fit. Apple created a cool product—but then the company just threw it at us and said: Here, you figure out why you need it.[2]

At the launch, Cook began right away by telling us the

product name and what it was. "So today I'm excited to announce an entirely new AR platform with a revolutionary new product. And here it is. Introducing Apple Vision Pro."

OK, then . . . why does the world need this? Next Cook said: "Vision Pro is a new kind of computer that augments reality by seamlessly blending the real world with a digital world. It's the first Apple product you look through and not at. Vision Pro feels familiar, yet it's entirely new. You can see, hear and interact with digital content just like it's in your physical space. And you can control Vision Pro using the most natural and intuitive tools, your eyes, hands, and voice."

But, again, Tim . . . why do we need it? What missing does it solve for? Cook kept going, next describing features:

"With Vision Pro, you're no longer limited by a display. Your surroundings become an infinite canvas. Use your apps anywhere and make them any size you want. Capture photos and videos and relive your most important memories in an entirely new way. Watch your movies, shows and sports, and immerse yourself in games on a giant screen surrounded by Spatial Audio. And connect with people as if you're sharing the same space. These are just some of the ways that Vision Pro blends digital content into the space around us."

At no time—not at the unveiling nor anytime over the next year—did Apple effectively lay out the context or the missing. It had an innovation it hoped would fulfill some kind of missing. It didn't see and create a market and develop an innovation to serve that market—it created a product and hoped it would find a market. The old Apple wouldn't have relied on us to do so much work figuring out why we would need what it was selling us. The post-Jobs Apple apparently forgot that.

In November 2024, Apple discontinued the Vision Pro.

How IKEA's Story Fit the Formula

The ideas behind the category creation formula have been around for ages, and the formula isn't just useful when dreaming up new technology. In fact, an old story—the story of IKEA and the emergence of the category of ready-to-assemble furniture—helped us see the formula.

For IKEA, the context was the rebuilding of Europe after World War II and the concurrent explosion of consumer purchases, including cars.

In his small Swedish town of Aggunaryd, Ingvar Kamprad started selling matches at age five to help make ends meet. After he graduated from school during the war in 1943, his father signed paperwork so the seventeen-year-old Kamprad could have a legal business, which he named IKEA, using his own initials and those of his farm, Elmtaryd, and town.[3]

The Swedish government was funding the construction of new houses and offering home furnishing loans. In 1948, Kamprad saw this emerging market and put out a mail order brochure featuring furniture from local manufacturers. He sold directly to consumers all over the Swedish countryside, and eventually moved from buying from local factories to making some of his own furniture.

At the same time, more and more people bought cars amid the postwar boom, and in Europe most of those cars were quite small—and not suited to transporting furniture.

One such car owner was an IKEA furniture designer named Gillis Lundgren. Lundgren bought a table, but he couldn't get it to fit in his car. Frustrated, Lundgren resorted to cutting off the legs to make the table fit, but that was obviously not a great solution to this problem. He recognized there was a missing that the context had created: Swedes were buying homes and cars and furniture—but that created a new problem of not being able to get the furniture to the home in the car.

Lundgren saw that this missing opened up an opportunity for an innovation: furniture made so it could be sold disassembled and packed flat to fit in cars.

This wasn't a completely new idea. Ready-to-assemble furniture first appeared in Europe around a hundred years before Lundgren sawed the legs off his table. However, that furniture was sold completely assembled but marketed as easy to take apart.

Lundgren's spin was to have the furniture already disassembled and easy to transport. He took his idea to Kamprad. The context plus missing plus innovation gave IKEA a chance to develop a new category of furniture.

Kamprad also realized that selling furniture that customers put together themselves could lower costs, making his furniture more affordable to a wider audience. When he added ready-to-assemble furniture to the company's catalog, the product line took off. A few years later, Kamprad opened a physical IKEA store so customers could see furniture already built, and leave with boxes that fit in their vehicles. The category flourished and IKEA became its undisputed leader.

While other producers saw IKEA's success and began to copy its model, they just helped IKEA by growing and evangelizing the category. That is the power of great category design, because it is very hard to unseat a category winner.

The ready-to-assemble furniture category has since caught on in places that were less impacted by the original problem. American cars might as well be aircraft carriers compared to the small European models Lundgren was familiar with. And yet, American consumers spent $13.8 billion in 2020 on ready-to-assemble furniture, largely because it can be good quality at low prices.

To see how ubiquitous IKEA has become, not just in the ready-to-assemble category but in the larger furniture market, you only have to look at the BILLY bookcase. Designed by Lundgren, this piece of furniture has sold over 60 million units worldwide. It is so popular that Bloomberg uses it as a pricing index to compare relative costs around the world.

Seventy years after its founding, IKEA had stores in fifty-two countries and was the largest furniture retailer in the world.

Here's a more modern story that shows how the category creation formula can lead to new market categories in old, established sectors.

It's the story of the Sports Bra, which isn't a women's bra. It's a bar in Portland, Oregon. Its owner developed a new category of bar.

Once again, if you look hard when there is a significant change in context, you can often see how that change in context is creating a new missing—something that should be there but isn't yet. Understanding that missing is a way to see an innovation that can solve for what's missing. Put it together, and you see a category to define and develop.

An incident in 2018 helped Jenny Nguyen recognize that a change in context showed her a missing she felt compelled to address. Nguyen had been a lifelong basketball nut and played for Clark College until she tore up her knee. Over the previous decade or so, the Women's National Basketball Association (WNBA), founded in 1996, had built up a significant fan base. At the same time, the US women's soccer team was often outdrawing the men's team at stadiums. The context around sports was shifting. More women (and men) than ever wanted to watch women's sports.

The incident that catalyzed Nguyen's thinking happened when she and a group of friends went to a nearly empty bar hoping to watch a women's college basketball championship game. They had to plead with the bartender to put the game on at least one of the bar's smallest TVs. If they'd gone to almost any sports bar, all the games on all their TVs would've been tuned to men's games. The clientele would've been dominated by men.

In that moment, Nguyen spotted this new missing that was not being addressed amid the context of the rising popularity of women's sports: There were no sports bars devoted to showing women's sports for a primarily female clientele.

That insight suggested the innovation: a women's sports bar for women.

Nguyen was also a restaurant chef, so she knew the business. She cobbled together enough savings, got a loan, fired up a Kickstarter campaign, and was able to fund the bar she felt compelled to create. It opened in 2022. Its TVs all showed women's sports. The walls were adorned with women's sports memorabilia. It sold booze made by women-owned distilleries. Its menu included vegan and gluten-free items. And the name was and is brilliant: the Sports Bra.

As Nguyen told CNBC: "The very first thing that came into my mind was The Sports Bra, and once I thought it, I couldn't un-think it, you know? It was catchy. I thought it was hilarious."*

In the Sports Bra's first eight months, it brought in $1 million in revenue. On many nights now, there are lines to get in. Nguyen hit a nerve—a category that matters. To put it another way, she identified a market that needed to be created, and built a product—her bar—to serve that market. She found market/product fit.

A healthy category needs more than one entrant. If you create a category and nobody follows you, you've probably created a category that doesn't matter. Before the Sports Bra's first year was up, a similar women's sports bar opened in Seattle. Then they started popping up in other cities. Nguyen told CNBC: "I would love to have as many people experience the feeling people experience when they walk through these doors. It feels very selfish to keep it to this one building that holds 40 people at a time."

Bars are an ancient category. There have long been all kinds of categories of bars: sports bars (for men), gay bars, cocktail bars, neighborhood bars. But there was still room for an innovative new category of bar.

And that can be said for any market sector. Context is always changing, and those shifts are always going to open up new missings that need new innovations. That doesn't just apply to technology. It can apply to anything—food, paint, razors, shoes, and on and on.

When Nguyen wrote her business plan, she got to the part about listing her competition. She said she thought about it for a minute and wrote: "The only competition is the status quo."

That should be a sentence every company aspires to write.

Following a major investment in the Sports Bra from Alexis Ohanian—cofounder of Reddit, founding control owner of Angel City FC, and founder of the 776 Foundation—the Sports Bra is expanding. In September 2024, the Sports Bra officially opened the opportunity to invest in a franchise. As Nguyen stated in *Forbes*, "Now, we are taking the next big step. It's time to invite others to join our team to bring The Sports Bra to communities across the country."[5]

How the Formula Helped LinkedIn See "Deep Sales"

We mentioned the LinkedIn Sales Solutions story earlier. The category creation formula played an important role in its category design journey.

In early 2022, we got a call from Gail Moody-Byrd, who had recently joined LinkedIn's Sales Solutions unit as VP of marketing. Moody-Byrd first met us when she was in her previous position as VP of marketing for Noodle.ai (now Daybreak), which had brought us in to help with category design a couple years earlier. LinkedIn had formed the Sales Solution unit around 2012, and it had developed a version of LinkedIn that would help sales professionals find and connect with potential customers. Ten years later, the unit's growth had slowed and competitors were chasing it, yet its leadership team believed the unit had the talent, technology, and data to create something new that would better serve a changing sales landscape.

Gail thought we could help, and so we took their leadership team through the category design process.

The category creation formula ended up being a turning point. The discussion it generated among the LinkedIn team surfaced new insights about the radically changing context around sales professionals. Those insights led them to what was missing and then to the innovation that the sales profession needed, a category of product LinkedIn labeled *deep sales*.

To illustrate the LinkedIn team's thinking, we're going to borrow here from a post that Gail published in September 2022.[6]

"The sales process has never been easy, but I've never seen it so broken for as many reasons as it is today," Gail wrote. "Too many sales professionals are stuck in what we've come to call 'shallow selling'—an endless, frustrating loop of contacting more and more potential buyers in ways that no longer work. Sales has been hit by a perfect storm of societal change and misguided technology. Once we at LinkedIn saw the problem, we couldn't unsee it."

She went on to describe many of the changes in context we discussed. The pandemic led to massive job changes. "One study found that 81% of sellers say that they have seen a deal lost or stalled because a buyer changed roles," Gail wrote. Buying had recently shifted from individuals to groups. "More than 80% of purchases now involve complex buying scenarios like consensus (in which three or more people are involved across two or more departments) and committees (in which strategic purchases include multiple people and departments across the organization and require executive oversight)." Meanwhile technology was making it easier to flood potential customers with spam and cold calls, which led to customers ignoring any communication that wasn't from an established relationship.

So the context was making sales professionals miserable. It had become harder to find the right people to sell to, harder to get through to them, and harder to develop relationships. That led the LinkedIn team to the missing: Sales professionals didn't have a product that would help them track potential customers, become useful to them in personalized ways, and build trust. The innovation would be to build a product that would help with that, and no other company was in a better position to do it than LinkedIn.

"What sales teams need now is a new category of sales technology called 'deep sales,'" Gail wrote. "Think of deep learning, where software learns from enormous amounts of reliable data to get to a meaningful answer. Deep sales relies on that kind of data to deeply understand buyers and their context." Of course, LinkedIn had that data and a product team that could deploy new, advanced AI to make it useful.

Deep sales gave LSS a new North Star. The division rallied around it. The product team built an innovative offering that solved for the missing. Marketers and LinkedIn sales people spread the word. The division's performance regained its mojo. Two years later, a study by Ipsos found that the new category of technology was working for sales professionals. "Sellers in the study who adopt the deep sales approach are nearly 2x more likely to beat their number versus shallow sellers," the study reported.[7]

Context + missing + innovation led LSS to a new market category it could define, design, develop, and ultimately win.

Why the Formula Is Valuable Right Now

As we write this in 2025, we believe it's never been more important for leadership teams to have sessions in which they discuss context + missing + innovation at least a couple of times a year. Or perhaps it should always be part of the conversation in every meeting about strategy, product road map, competition, and positioning.

Why? Because this is a time of extraordinary changes in context, and great changes in context open up more missings.

Stay on top of context shifts, and your team will see opportunities to create new market categories.

In 2018, Hemant Taneja, CEO of investment company General Catalyst, and Kevin published a book titled *Unscaled: How AI and a New Generation of Upstarts Are Creating the Economy of the Future*. Its premise rests on the historical arc of innovation over the previous 130 years.[8]

Between 1890 and 1920, the world experienced an unprecedented wave of technological innovation. In those years, the US saw the electrification of much of the country, the spread of Alexander Graham Bell's telephones, the first radio broadcasts, the first powered flight by the Wright brothers, and, with the Ford Model T, the arrival of mass-market automobiles. These were all foundational technologies. That is, they didn't do just one thing; they opened paths for all manner of innovation and change. For instance, electricity, transportation, and communication allowed factories to scale up and mass-produce goods, which made everything from food to furniture cheaper and more abundant.

In every way, life transformed dramatically between 1890 and 1920. A lot of the changes were for the better, lifting millions out of poverty, freeing people from farm labor, adding decades to life expectancy, and generally making existence easier. But they also exacerbated gulfs between rich and poor, between management and labor, and between people with fundamentally different views of how society should be organized. Geopolitical power shifted from Europe to the US. Cultural change (Flappers! Jazz! Women's suffrage! Prohibition!) blew through society.

It was all driven by the day's emerging technologies, and such enormous change teed the world up for instability. As Hemant and Kevin wrote in *Unscaled*: "Not to be alarmist, but in the early 1900s—the last time technology so completely transformed the economy and life—the shocks were followed by two world wars, a global economic depression, and the rise of a Western-led liberal world order."

The remaining decades of the twentieth century certainly saw lots of technological innovations, but they were never as clustered, intense, or profound as in that 1890 to 1920 period.

Then, in 2007, Apple introduced its iPhone—in a way, the Model T of the twenty-first century. And by now, much of the world's population has a remarkably powerful computer in its pocket. Also in 2007: Amazon rolled out Amazon Web Services (AWS), and cloud computing fully arrived, allowing people to access software, services, and content anywhere, anytime. Social networks became ubiquitous, fundamentally changing the nature of community and communication. (Facebook was founded in 2004; Twitter, now X, in 2006.)

We're being overwhelmed by a tsunami of new foundational technology. Now, more than ever, artificial intelligence is allowing computer systems to learn and to solve problems that humans can't. AI is in the process of transforming every single industry. At the same time, in biotechnology, the CRISPR technique is enabling scientists to edit genes and program DNA. Blockchain has brought new ways to think about money, contracts, and identity. The list of paradigm-shifting innovations goes on, and includes 3D printing, virtual reality, the metaverse, and civilian space flight.

When such a wave comes, it doesn't just alter a behavior or two. It changes everything. Economist Carlota Perez described the impact of such moments in time in her influential 2003 book, *Technological Revolutions and Financial Capital: The Dynamics of Bubbles and Golden Ages*: "When a technological revolution irrupts in the scene, it does not just add some dynamic new industries to the previous production structure. It provides the means for modernizing all the existing industries and activities."[9]

So yes, we are in the midst of "modernizing all the existing industries and activities."

That means enormous, wrenching, society-overhauling change. We see it all around us. Part of society is racing ahead with cryptocurrencies, social media, AI, and on and on—while others fight to hold on to a way of life they've always known. So divides widen in society and politics, and between rich and poor, and rising and falling nations. That leads to civil unrest and, yes, wars.

If the past is prologue, we are halfway through our thirty-year cycle of technological revolution. As AI, crypto, gene editing, and other technologies mature and accelerate changes, there's a good chance that they will lead to the continued ripping up of social and economic norms and geopolitical maps. In other words, brace yourself for more of the kind of turmoil we're experiencing now.

And yet, imagine all the opportunities these foundational technologies are creating. We can reinvent every industry and everything about the way we live. The next decade may see the arrival of universal, cheap, clean energy and AI-driven technology that reverses climate change. We may fix our genes so that we live to one hundred with thirty-year-old bodies. We may see a complete realignment of nations that secures peace and lifts up poorer countries. We could be buzzing around in flying cars, spending much of our time in the metaverse, and vacationing in space hotels. We'll do a lot of things that are beyond our conception today.

Sometime in the next fifteen years, this revolution will hit a turning point and shift into a phase "leading ultimately to a different 'way of life,'" as Perez stated. That's where we finally arrived after World War II. For the seventy years that followed, the Western world was relatively peaceful, creating a modern life unimaginable to anyone alive in 1890—a life of cars, TVs, supermarkets, advanced health care, jet travel, computers, professional sports, and skyscrapers.

Innovators have a generational chance to reinvent industries and daily life in beneficial ways. One way to see how to do that is through the category creation formula.

5

The Adjacent Possible

In 2010, Steven Johnson published the book *Where Good Ideas Come From: The Natural History of Innovation*. It's a study of the patterns throughout history that lead to an explosive moment when an innovation—such as the pencil, flush toilet, or battery—catches on and changes the way we work or live. To us, as category designers, the most important concept in the book is what Johnson called the *adjacent possible*.[1]

Johnson borrowed the concept from biology and modified it for his purposes. We, in turn, borrowed it from Johnson and modified it for strategic category design purposes. The adjacent possible has become a key to unlocking clarity about a company's category and long-term vision.

In the book, Johnson tries to understand why certain innovations take hold and change the world at that one particular moment in time. The adjacent possible helps explain that. The concept divides innovations into two categories: the "possible" and the "not-yet-possible." The possible are things that already exist and work and are understood and adopted by the market. The not-yet-possible are, essentially, lab experiments and dreams—technology that doesn't yet work well and that the broad market hasn't adopted and probably doesn't understand. Today, for instance, mass-market electric cars land in the possible. Flying cars in every driveway land in the not-yet-possible. (Getting closer, but not yet!)

The adjacent possible is a thin band between these two zones. Innovations change the world when they land there. Such innovations stretch the possible beyond where it's been before, but not so much that the technology doesn't work or we can't understand it.

Johnson argues that a key factor in hitting this sweet spot is that technologies and a zeitgeist that can support the innovation are already well-developed. The innovation can add a discovery or missing piece and build on what's already there, so it seems new yet works and is readily adoptable.

For example, when the Wright brothers first flew in 1903, all the mechanics and theories necessary—from the piston engine to wing aerodynamics—already existed. The Wrights just had to push the technology a bit further by putting the right parts together and adding some key insights of their own. By that point, too, early cars were on roads and inventors had been trying for years to fly, so the public was ready to believe a machine could do this. Twenty years earlier, an airplane would've seemed like science fiction to most people. But twenty years after the flight at Kitty Hawk, airplanes were embraced by the public.

In strategic category design, we modify the model just a bit. We give equal weight to what technology can do and what society can accept—an acknowledgment that the capabilities of technology often get ahead of most people's ability to adopt that technology and make use of it.

In our model, the capabilities of technology are represented on the vertical axis. Society's ability to adopt a technology is on the horizontal axis. (See figure below.) Possible innovations are in the dark-gray zone. Not-yet-possible innovations land in the light gray zone. The adjacent possible is the white band between. Keep in mind that the white band constantly moves out over time as new technologies get invented and society becomes used to them.

New categories of products and services take hold and scale when they hit the adjacent possible. The dark-gray space is where you'd find categories that already exist and

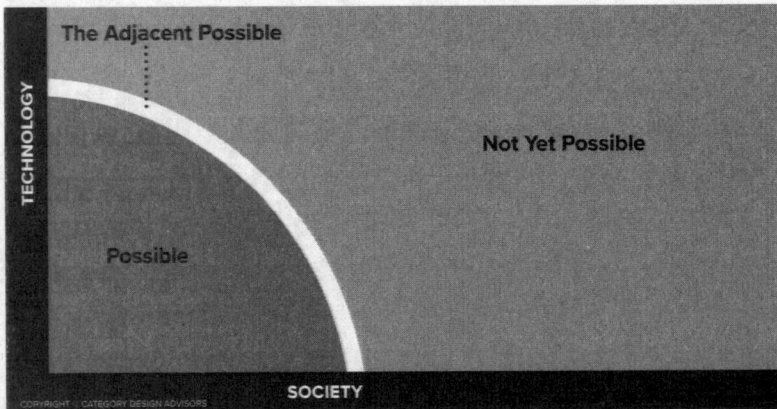

are widely adopted—and in all likelihood, those are categories where the category winner has been decided. If a company's product or service lands in the dark gray, the company will forever wind up trying to whittle away market share held by the category leader.

The light-gray space is where you'd find categories that are not ready for prime time. If a company's product or service lands in the light gray, the company is out ahead of either technological capabilities or most of society's interest in adopting that category—or, usually, both. Land too far into the light gray, and you very well could end up as one of those companies with a supercool, futuristic vision—that then runs out of money and time before becoming a sustainable business.

When we're working with a company on strategic category design, we'll put up a slide showing the adjacent possible graph and start a discussion about where that company's offerings would land. This is something every leadership team can do whenever discussing strategy and product road map.

As you might imagine, the goal should be to land right now in the adjacent possible.

If you find you're in the dark-gray space, you'd have to acknowledge that you're in an existing, decided category. That means your company has two options. One is to commit to staying there. Millions of businesses around the world are started in existing categories with a goal of winning some market share by competing on features or price. The other option—the category designer option—is to push your vision and offering beyond the dark-gray space, out to the adjacent possible, where you have a chance of creating a new market category, or competing to win a still-emerging category.

Or, you may look at the adjacent possible graph and realize your company lands in the light gray space. The good news is that you're probably out ahead of the competition. You are creating a market category from scratch with unproven technology, and it might seem like science fiction to most people.

Again, you have two options.

One is to develop a version of your offering that may not fulfill your vision, but lands in the adjacent possible today, with a road map to eventually get to your vision as technology and society advance. The other option only works if you're in the light gray but close to the adjacent possible, and that is to try to pull the adjacent possible line toward you. To do that, you'll have to offer a breakthrough innovation that really works while at the same time aggressively educating the market so it understands and adopts what you're creating.

If you're far out into the light gray, there's one bad decision you can make: to stubbornly stay there and stick to your vision. Those kinds of companies are the ones we admire for helping us imagine the future, and they're the kinds of companies that disappear before that future happens.

Real Dangers of Missing the Adjacent Possible

Our friend and a coauthor of *Play Bigger*, Al Ramadan, experienced firsthand the difficulty of being on the wrong side of the adjacent possible.

When you tune in to coverage of, say, the Olympics or a Formula One race, you probably take for granted all the cool graphics and detailed data that you see on the screen—how fast sprinters run, how a play developed in basketball, the rpm and speed of a race car. In the mid-1990s, that stuff didn't yet exist for audiences. But it was envisioned and predicted by a Silicon Valley company most people don't remember, called Quokka Sports. Al was its CEO.[2]

Kevin first visited Quokka in 1998. The company was mostly focused on covering competitive sailing. But even then, the company had a grand vision for a future of digital immersive sports.

The consumer internet was new back then. The vast majority of people who were getting on it were doing so via painfully slow dial-up modems. It took forever just to download a photo. Video was pretty much out of the question.

Al, who had majored in computer science at Monash University, was an intense athlete who got involved in sailing. In 1992, Al was asked by Australian sailing legend John Bertrand to be chief technologist for Bertrand's upcoming run at the America's Cup yacht race. As Al told Kevin then, Bertrand thought digital technology could give a sailing team an edge. So the team packed its boat with sensors that could send fifty variables to a computer, which in turn could track and analyze the incoming data.

"I'd be standing there during the race with all this information coming into my computer, and I realized all these people were gathered around me watching my screen instead of watching the boats," Al told Kevin during a 1998 interview. He realized the onlookers were experiencing a different version of yacht racing than they'd ever seen—an intimate view of a sport that is otherwise far away out on the sea. What if that kind of experience could be available to the public—for sailing or any sport?

After the 1995 America's Cup (won by New Zealand), Al went to Stanford to take a summer MBA course. The consumer internet was just getting going. Al and Bertrand made plans for a company that could use the internet to cover yacht racing in this new data-intensive way. Eric Schmidt—later of Google fame but then at Sun Microsystems—introduced those two to veteran technologist Dick Williams. Al, Bertrand, and Williams founded Quokka in 1996.

More recently, Al looked back: "Quokka was one of the hottest tech companies in the Valley in the mid–late 1990s. Investors included Accel Partners, Media Technology Ventures, Intel Capital, Liberty Media, NBC. It was the mixing of data overlays with live video coupled with interactivity that delivered a new lens on the sporting event. If people were into the 'story,' they could hear it from the athlete—no reporter in between. If they were into the stats, they could download our Race Viewer, which gave you a million options to view the event."

By the late 1990s, every entity on earth wanted to get in on the dot-com boom, and that included NBC, which had the rights to the 2000 Summer Olympics. Yacht racing proved the concept, but NBC realized that what Quokka was doing could work for other sports. Quokka and NBC created NBCOlympics.com, the first internet site to cover the Olympics live. Quokka layered data into coverage of thirty-five sports, such as swimming and track.

So what happened to Quokka?

It was a classic case of getting too far ahead of the adjacent possible. Technology and the public didn't catch up to Quokka's vision in time. In 2000, internet connections were still too slow for a good video experience, and much of the audience just wasn't used to looking online to watch sports—a chicken-and-egg problem. The great dot-com crash that started in 2000 devastated Quokka's stock price and soured investors on internet companies.

In 2002, Quokka folded. As Al has said many times, if Quokka had been able to get through the storm of those years, today it might be a sports media giant. Instead, the company disappeared—but everything it envisioned came true.

Nobody was talking about the adjacent possible in the 1990s. It might have led the Quokka team to make some different strategic decisions—ones that would've helped the company land in the adjacent possible in time to save it from going under.

Too many entrepreneurs, technologists, and investors still don't pay heed to the adjacent possible.

The most recent big whiff, as mentioned earlier, is the Humane Ai Pin. *The New York Times* did a terrific job of describing what it's supposed to be: The two founders, who came from Apple, "set out to create a lapel pin that clips to clothing with a magnet. The device gives users access to an AI-powered virtual assistant that can send messages, search the web or take photos. It is complemented by a laser that projects text onto the palm of a user's hand for tasks like skipping a song while playing music. It also has a camera, a speaker and cellular service."[3]

Salesforce CEO Marc Benioff invested. So did OpenAI chief Sam Altman. SoftBank and Tiger Global pitched in. The company raised more than $230 million. They all apparently bought into the idea that AI pins would disrupt and replace smartphones.

But it failed the adjacent possible test.

From the very first demos of Humane's Ai Pin, it seemed obvious it was too far into the light gray (i.e., it wouldn't gain traction in the near future). The company struggled to make the technology work (tech too far into the light gray). People in general are still quite enamored with their smartphones and so are years away from understanding why they'd want an AI pin to replace those phones (society too far into the light gray). As a result, Humane found no real market to sell into, and no healthy ecosystem of suppliers, developers, and partners. The company started sputtering, top executives left, and the press ate it alive. In early 2025 the company ceased to exist. Some of its assets were bought by HP for $116 million—about one-third of the amount of money investors had put in.

When discussing strategy and the adjacent possible, it's always important to pay attention to what both the technology and society can support. We've often encountered technical founders who are jazzed about the breakthrough they've developed, but forget that if they can't land it in the adjacent possible line, whatever they've built won't get accepted.

Here's another case in point from the sports technology universe, somewhat related to Quokka.

The Fox TV network signed up to start broadcasting NHL games in 1995—the first time hockey would be on network television since 1974. Executives at Fox were worried that Americans were either too ignorant of hockey or too blind to follow the puck (or both) on a TV screen.

To be fair, 1995 tube TVs were nothing like today's high-definition ones. Some TV visuals were so fuzzy, if you had the sound off, it could be hard to tell if you were watching *Friends* or a congressional hearing. "One of the biggest complaints about hockey on TV is, 'I can't see the puck!'" a Fox spokesperson, Vince Wladika, said back then.[4]

This was long before electronics did much to enhance our sports viewing—before we could instantly see if a pitcher hit the strike zone; before soccer players wore chips that track their movements on the field; before cameras and AI could tell if a tennis shot landed inside the line.

Among the TV networks at the time, Fox prided itself on innovation. So Fox started looking at embedding microprocessors in pucks, which would allow computers to superimpose graphics over the puck in order to make it easier to follow. In early 1996, it was ready. Fox branded this electronic puck as FoxTrax.

To make it work, Fox cut pucks in half lengthwise, scraped out a little cavity in the middle, and inserted a bunch of electronics that could generate thirty infrared pulses a second.

Tiny holes around the ridge of the puck let the pulses out. A network of infrared sensors placed around the rink would pick up the pulses and track the puck. The puck had to be glued back together with super-adhesive. "We tested that by shooting pucks out of cannons at a wall, and none ever failed," a Fox VP said.

Older hockey fans may remember what happened next. Fox used the puck-tracking to make the puck glow with a blue halo around it. This was Fox's answer to helping viewers see the puck better. Then, when a player took a shot, an orange comet tail would swoosh behind the puck.

Neither seemed to do much to pull in new hockey fans, and the hockey faithful thought it was awful. It turned a game into a combination of live action and cartoon—as if a hockey game broke out during the *Who Framed Roger Rabbit* movie. Greg Wyshynski, editor of *Yahoo! Sports'* long-dead *Puck Daddy* blog, once told a journalist: "Imagine if you were watching the Super Bowl and every time the running back disappeared in a pile of tacklers he started glowing like a blueberry from Chernobyl."

Fox didn't actually kill off its compu-puck. In 1998, Fox lost the NHL broadcast rights to ABC, and FoxTrax disappeared. ABC apparently didn't have any desire to use glowing pucks.

Looking back now, FoxTrax defied the adjacent possible. The technology was crude. The target market didn't want it. Yet.

The creators of FoxTrax left Fox and started the company Sportvision, knowing that the basic idea of using electronics to enhance sports viewing would eventually be right. In time, Sportvision created the baseball pitch trackers we now see on every broadcast, the yellow first-down lines on NFL broadcasts, and a bunch of stuff for Olympic events. The company was later acquired by SMT. Once high-definition TVs hit the market, the need to artificially enhance the visibility of pucks for NHL games faded away. Instead, technology now can track pucks and players, generating data and probabilities that coaches can use for training and tactics.

The technology got better. The public embraced it. The innovations landed in the adjacent possible and caught on. By now, technology-enhanced sports viewing has passed into the realm of existing market categories.

The Innovation Spectrum

Related to the concept of the adjacent possible is another thinking tool about innovation that we call the innovation spectrum.

The spectrum we're talking about ranges from *hierarchical* at one end to *emergent* on the other end. Knowing where your innovation lands on that spectrum can inform you about how to approach investors, what kind of product to build now versus later, and how you'll defend the company against competitors that eventually come into the category.

Similar to the roots of the adjacent possible, the concepts of emergent and hierarchical are more common in biology and physics. We first learned about it from yet another book by Steven Johnson, titled *Emergence: The Connected Lives of Ants, Brains, Cities, and Software.*[5]

We got thinking about those concepts after a discussion with a company's founders about what kind of product they should build first. The company had a huge vision but knew it couldn't create that vision all at once. It rightly decided to begin with a product that would give any early user an immediate "aha!" moment—a more emergent than hierarchical approach.

First, an explanation of the terms and their properties as they apply to technology and innovation.

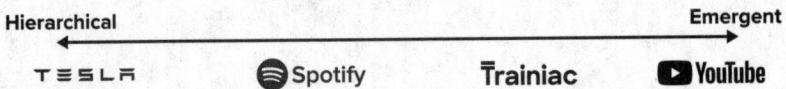

Hierarchical ← ——————————————————————— → **Emergent**

TΞSLⅎ   Spotify   Trainiac   ▶ YouTube

At one extreme end of the innovation spectrum are highly hierarchical innovations. These are complex products or services that need to be built completely, according to a master plan, before the first customer gets anything out of it.

One example of that is Tesla. The company had to design a whole electric car, develop an ecosystem of suppliers, build a factory, hire a lot of people, design a way for the cars to get charged, and create a way to sell and service the cars before the first real customer could buy a Tesla and be satisfied with it.

Such a highly hierarchical innovation requires an enormous investment and a lot of time before getting traction. That may sound like a downside, but it can be an advantage. If the innovation is right—if it works and the market wants it and the timing is on target—then the huge investment of money and time becomes a big barrier to entry for competitors.

So a hierarchical innovation that is right can become highly valuable, as has happened with Tesla. Tesla created a new category of electric cars and got a long head start over competitors. Investors have understood that, which is why Tesla in mid-2024 was valued at $724 billion while Ford was valued at $44 billion.[6]

Other examples of successful category-creating, highly hierarchical innovations include the Boeing 707 (first jetliner), IBM System/360 (first mainframe product line), Apple's iPhone, and OpenAI's ChatGPT. The 707 and 360 were such giant investments, they were literally bet-the-company projects.

But here's the catch: The delta between being right and wrong about a highly hierarchical innovation is huge. Get it right, and you could rake in billions of dollars. Get it wrong, and you may not know it's wrong for years while in development. By the time the innovation fails to work or catch on, you've lost ungodly amounts of money, time, and effort—or maybe killed the company.

Over the years, we've seen quite a few got-it-wrong calamities in tech. General Magic, Iridium, Teledesic, and Webvan are examples. In each case, a vast system had to be built before the first customers could use it. In each case, the technology and timing were wrong—running afoul of the adjacent possible—and those companies' implosions left craters.

At the other end of the continuum are highly emergent innovations.

These start out simply and can be initially built with a small investment and little time. The first customer can find an early version immediately useful, although in a limited way. If it's emergent, the innovation has a future to grow into. Over time it attracts more users, developers, and partners that continue to add to the innovation and make it more valuable to everyone involved.

An example of that is YouTube. It was first conceived as an easy way for someone to share a video with friends and family. Before YouTube, sites like Flickr let people share photos, but the same capability didn't exist for videos. In 2005, YouTube's founders, Steve Chen, Chad Hurley, and Jawed Karim, built and launched a beta version in about three months, and the first users started uploading their videos. There wasn't much to the site.

As more people added more videos and yet more people came to the site to see them, YouTube grew more valuable and robust, evolving into a media giant that now includes live TV, full-length movies, and people who've gotten rich doing nothing but making YouTube videos. Imagine how hard it would've been to build all of that at the outset before letting the first customer in.

A lot of tech successes have leaned toward the emergent side. Amazon didn't start by building warehouses and stocking vast numbers of items and creating its own logistics system. At first it just sold books (which it would buy directly from publishers and rare book dealers) and sent them to customers by mail or UPS. Facebook started as an online student directory at Harvard. Uber started as an app for hailing a black car only in San Francisco.

Highly emergent innovations have their own upsides and downsides for category creators. An upside is that they take relatively little money and time to build, so an idea can get launched quickly with a small team.

But that's also a downside. If an innovation opens up a category that matters, it won't take much for competitors to rush in and catch up. Competitive advantage only takes hold once the innovation has attracted so many users, developers, and partners that together they make the system highly valuable for everyone involved and no one has a reason to go to any competitor.

For a highly emergent innovation, the delta between being right and wrong at the outset is relatively tiny. Get it right, and it's not that valuable at first. Get it wrong, and you've only lost a little time and money, and haven't built anything so complex that you can't adjust and pivot.

Interestingly, either way—hierarchical or emergent—it takes years of dedicated work to fully design, develop, and win the new category you're creating. For a hierarchical innovation, that work takes place out of the public eye and then, suddenly, a full-blown product is ready. For an emergent innovation, the early product has to iterate bit by bit and add users and an ecosystem, evolving into a robust, category-defining product. Everyone involved sees and participates in the progress along the way.

Importantly, this is a spectrum. If you put Tesla at one end and YouTube at the other, there's a range of possibilities in between. As you move along the innovation spectrum, you dial up and down the various advantages and disadvantages.

Perhaps the innovation you want to build has to be mostly complete before users get value, but it's not as heavy a lift as building a Tesla or ChatGPT. Spotify comes to mind. It had to build a platform and license a lot of music before early users would find it valuable.

Or you're creating something that leans toward emergent but requires some robustness before launching. One of our clients, Trainiac, had to build a smart fitness app and also develop a network of personal trainers before getting its first users. It wasn't a superheavy lift, but it took some time and investment, and at launch Trainiac had a slight lead over anyone else that might come into its category.

How does all of this play a role in building a category-defining company?

Where you land on the spectrum tells something about how much you'll have to raise before producing revenue. If you're highly hierarchical, you'll have to raise a lot and do a ton of work to convince investors you're right.

If your innovation is highly emergent, you can start with little funding and quickly get a lightweight product out the door, but it's important to make sure you show investors how you can build on that so it becomes a much bigger business over time.

Many companies know from the beginning whether they are building something hugely ambitious that will take time and money, or a product that can start small and emerge over time. But if you're an early-stage startup with a monster break-through vision that will likely take years to come true, look at options along the continuum. You may find you can quickly get an emergent product out the door, then build on it bit by bit.

The innovation spectrum can also help you know what battles you'll have to fight. For a highly hierarchical product, your chief competition is likely yourself. If you're right and if you're an outlier (no one else is building the same thing), you could have quite a bit of time before challengers pop up. Emergent innovations can be more easily challenged. Then the task is to keep evolving the product ahead of competitors and setting the expectations for how the category of product should work.

The innovation spectrum also tells you a type of innovation to avoid: one that is neither hierarchical nor emergent.

A lot of stand-alone phone apps fall into this category, like an alarm clock app. It's relatively simple to build and quickly gives a user satisfaction, so it's not hierarchical, but it's also not emergent—there's not much to build on to lure users, developers, and partners.

An innovation that doesn't seem to be either emergent or hierarchical will likely never win a market category and become valuable.

Mike's Hard Lesson in Hierarchical Innovation

One of your authors, Mike, found out firsthand what it's like to be right about the category, too early for the adjacent possible, and too optimistic about the burden of building a very hierarchical product.

In the mid-1990s, Mike was working for a software company called Modicon. To help streamline Modicon's sales process, he developed a product configurator tool in Microsoft Excel. One of the company's investors told Mike that the configurator seemed like a new kind of technology—a new category. That encouraged Mike to leave Modicon and start a company, Pangaea, to create what would be the category of product configuration software.

To make the product work, it needed artificial intelligence, which was then not well-developed or particularly useful. Plus, enterprise software ecosystems were far from ready to support such innovation. That meant Pangaea had to build not only its software product but also the surrounding infrastructure, including the AI—an enormous lift for a startup. Hierarchical innovations like Pangaea's need massive investment and extended development timelines, and that leaves little room for iterative learning or market adjustment. And while the technology was visionary, it was too early, and customers weren't ready for it. Early customers required significant customization and consulting, further slowing progress.

You can guess where this story is going. Without the infrastructure or societal readiness to support the category, Pangaea's vision was not gaining traction fast enough. The company burned through its investment capital. Eventually, the category—which took on the label *configure price quote*, or CPQ—was right, and the technology got built. Today, CPQ is a busy, thriving category, with a market valued at $3 billion in 2025, with projections that it will grow to $7 billion by 2030.[7]

But Pangaea ran out of resources and was forced to pivot to a more traditional enterprise-consulting model. This decision, driven by investor pressure, shifted the company from category creation to direct competition with established consulting. That proved to be Pangaea's undoing. In 2000, the company shuttered its doors.

The Right Mix: Practical Visionaries

The concepts of the adjacent possible and the innovation spectrum are not meant to discourage visionaries. Our civilization needs them and always has.

We needed Quokka and Fox to give us an early glimpse of what sports entertainment could look like, even if technology and/or society weren't there yet. We needed General Magic to dangle ideas about what the internet might be, even if it was way too early and way too hierarchical for one company to pull off. Visionaries help us see things we never thought of before. They set new goals for scientists and engineers to build to. They make the public hungry for what might come next. It's how progress happens.

But the visionaries who really matter are "practical visionaries."

A practical visionary wants to take technology and society to a new place on the frontier, but also understands how to get there from today.

Practical visionaries look at the adjacent possible graph, see that their goal is to build something out into the light gray, and find a way to ratchet back to the adjacent possible now so their companies become sustainable and will stick around to take us on a journey to the future.

Practical visionaries know where their breakthrough lands on the innovation spectrum, and they find a way to either start small and emerge toward the future one step at a time . . . or go bold and get the backing and time necessary to build a hierarchical system that lands us in the future in one giant leap.

Practical visionaries deploy all the tools of strategic category design to make sure their innovation creates a market and brings others into the category so it becomes robust. Category design helps practical visionaries set the rules for their innovation, so others don't grab the category's steering wheel and take the category in an unwanted direction. Category design helps practical visionaries keep vision entropy at bay, aligning the team and other stakeholders around a shared goal.

Practical visionaries create important new categories— the ones that pull us out of the mere possible and take us somewhere new. Strategic category design is a grounded, applicable way for visionaries to make sure their dreams become reality.

6

The Secret Life
of Categories

You may have ideas about what drove the BlackBerry into extinction even though businesspeople adored using the device and its tiny keyboard for email. Or why a whole bunch of other mobile device form factors, operating systems, and brands got wiped off the planet within a few years of Apple introducing the iPhone in 2007.

But all that can be better understood by viewing it through the lens of an economist's brilliant theory about how new, innovative market categories come to life, develop, and mature over time.

You can read about that theory in the book *The Evolution of New Markets*, by economist Paul Geroski.[1] We borrow a lot from Geroski in our strategic category design practice.

In fact, we're generally flummoxed about why his book is not better known. Geroski's study of the behavior of market categories can help every leadership team think about strategy, positioning, innovation, competition, and their organization's ultimate mission.

And you can get a good understanding of the most important concepts in Geroski's work, and how it applies to category design, through the story of the smartphone category.

Paul Geroski was born in the US but spent most of his adult life in the UK, first as a professor at several universities and then as chair of the UK's Competition Commission. (Geroski died of cancer in 2005 at age fifty-two. We wish he were around so we could talk to him about all this.)

Geroski based his initial research on the automobile industry. Once Geroski understood the dynamic in the automobile category, he studied other market categories and realized that the same pattern tends to play out again and again. In fact, the pattern must play out in order for a new category to develop.

The heart and soul of Geroski's thinking about the evolution of market categories is a simple graph (see following page).

It's really two graphs overlapping. We'll start with the first, showing the number of companies in a market category—the solid line in the chart.

The bottom left corner marks the moment when a new market category is born. That typically happens when a meaningful innovation first surfaces. At that point, the innovation to most people probably seems strange or hard to understand, or even like science fiction. It's pushing the adjacent possible. There may be just one company in the space—the

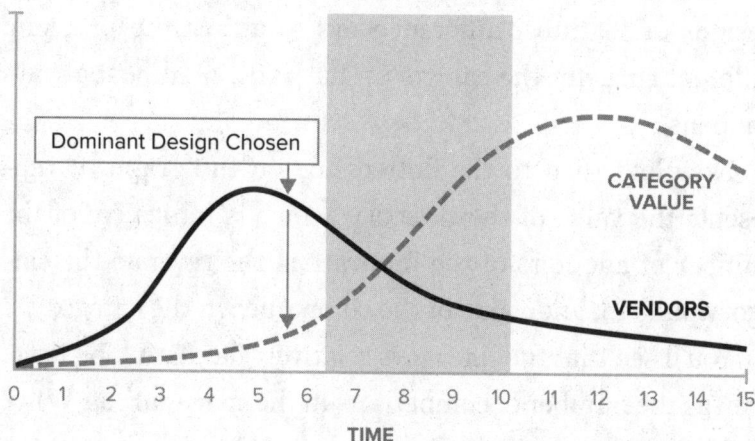

Dominant Design Chosen

CATEGORY
VALUE

VENDORS

0 1 2 3 4 5 6 7 8 9 10 11 12 13 14 15

TIME

SOURCE: PAUL GEROSKI

one that came up with the innovation. And there are very few users—maybe just friends and family.

As Geroski wrote: "New radical innovations create new markets: they serve needs that have not yet been served by any good or service, or they meet existing needs in radically new ways. Either way, before they are developed there is no well-defined market for them to be sold into and, hence, no demand signals of this sort exist to stimulate their development."

Follow the solid line from left to right. If this new category of innovation looks promising—if the world really needs it to exist—competitors start piling in, believing that demand will appear. The number of companies in the space rises. This is the sign of a category that is going to matter. If nobody else follows the category creator into the category, it's probably a category that won't matter.

A lot of competing companies barge into the space with somewhat different versions of the innovation—different designs or features, different ways to attack the problem, different rules for the category. That's OK—it almost always happens.

Now let's turn to the dotted line on the graph. It represents the value of the category, which is indicative of the number of adopters of the innovation, the revenue the category pulls in, and value of the companies in the category.

You'll see that the line stays relatively flat for a long time, even as the number of competitors in the space surges. Why? In the first chaotic years of a category, early adopters test the waters but the larger market sits on the sidelines. Most people at this point are trying to figure out how this new thing fits into the way they work or live and are wondering which version will be the right one to buy.[2]

If you keep following the lines from left to right, you'll see a dramatic shift. At a similar moment in time, the number of companies in the category plunges (solid line) while the value of the category rockets (dotted line).

The driver of that shift is the emergence of the category's *dominant design*—to use Geroski's term. This is enormously important in strategic category design.

At some moment in a category's life, the market decides that one design is the winner. Geroski shows that it's the nature of any category to consolidate around a dominant design. The reasons are many. Buyers don't want to sort through a lot of competing designs to decide what to use and then worry that the one they choose will get usurped. A dominant design also helps an ecosystem form. Suppliers, developers, and partners know what to build for and know they're not going to waste time building for a version that's soon to go defunct. Economies of scale kick in, too, which is not possible when competitors are all producing different versions for niche groups of customers.

Oddly, though, Geroski found no way to pinpoint why a particular design wins the dominant design or when it happens.

In some cases, the winning design is clearly superior—but not always. Other times, Geroski argued, a company's lesser design wins because that company does a great job convincing people that it should win and that the choice had already been made for them. (Which, right there, describes the purpose of category design.)

As Geroski noted in his book: "A dominant design will emerge when it becomes clear that the majority of consumers are content for a particular design to be selected, when a bandwagon forms that focuses the choices of consumers on a single particular design."

The solidifying of a dominant design changes everything for a category. The mass market—whether consumer or business-to-business (B2B)—feels safe adopting that new innovation. Buyers believe the product won't disappear or quickly become outmoded. A supporting ecosystem grows around that version of the innovation. All in all, the broader universe of buyers—those who have been standing by and watching—rushes in, and the economics of the category accelerate upward.

As the dominant design takes hold, the number of companies in the space collapses as competitors lose out, get acquired, or join the dominant ecosystem. This goes on until just a few companies remain—typically a clear category winner that controls the dominant design, followed by no more than a few lesser contenders.

"The outcome of this consolidation process often comes to define the market," Geroski wrote. "It yields a well-defined, widely recognized product, and (typically) a small set of associated producers who form the backbone of pretty much everything that happens thereafter."

The dominant design is a profound moment of transformation for a category. And then what happens many years after the dominant design drives consolidation? As the category matures, a dominant company followed by a few others captures almost all the demand for that product or service. Any new entrant finds it extremely difficult to barge in and take significant market share. Over time, the category's growth tails off, innovation becomes incremental, and the companies in the category milk their offerings for as long as they can.

That life cycle has played out over and over in category after category. Geroski, as mentioned, started by studying automobiles. As his theory would predict, the first cars appeared in the late 1890s. By 1910, there were 485 car companies, all making different designs. In 1908, Henry Ford produced the Model T. Within a few years a dominant design similar to the Model T took hold and the market consolidated, eventually down to just three major automakers in the US.

The pattern has held for consumer electronics, software, food, airplanes, and just about every other sector.

Which brings us to smartphones. . . .

The Geroski Lens on the Smartphone Category

In 1983, there were a total of 1,000 cell phones in the US. In 1984, the number exploded to 100,000; in 1985, it hit 200,000. The category of cell phone was just getting established. Most people had no idea what cell phones would be good for. Back then, in a story he wrote for *USA Today*, Kevin quoted a trade publication editor named Stuart Crump as saying: "Why don't people buy cellular phones? It's not yet in their frame of reference. It's not in their thought pattern. That's the problem to overcome."[3]

Early cell phones cost about $1,000, which would be about $2,800 today. Calls cost 45 cents a minute. In 1985, the phone company in California at the time, Pacific Telesis, gave Kevin a portable cell phone to try out. It was the size of a small overnight suitcase. It rode on the passenger seat as he drove around Los Angeles in a rental car trying to make calls. Most of the time, it was like trying to make a call from the dark side of the moon. It broke up constantly.

Cellular phones evolved slowly over the next five years or so. Truly usable cell phones started appearing in the late 1990s, driven by Nokia and Motorola introducing some of the first that fit in a pocket. Cell systems were good enough, the cost to use them was dropping, and the public started understanding that it was pretty useful to make calls while stuck in traffic or watching your kid's soccer game.

That initial category of cell phone was all about making voice calls. For quite a long time, no one thought these devices were good for anything else. When the BlackBerry first came out, for instance, it was a separate device that only did email. Palm Computing offered the PalmPilot handheld device, but at first it had no wireless connection—you had to plug it into a personal computer to update information on it. Analog, voice-centric cell phones could send texts, but you had to painfully type using the numeric telephone keypad.

And yet, around the fringes, technologists started envisioning a blending of voice, text, and internet connection. In 1994, IBM and BellSouth teamed up to create the Simon, usually considered the first crossover smartphone. It was long and clunky and had a monochrome screen that couldn't do much. But it seeded the idea of a new category of smartphone. You could place the Simon on the bottom left corner of a Geroski graph.

In the early 2000s, the number of vendors moved upward in earnest. New takes on the smartphone concept were created by Palm's successor, Handspring, and by Nokia in Finland and Kyocera in Japan. They all had different form factors and different operating systems. If you got familiar with one and then bought a different brand, you had to learn all over again how to use it. Connecting to the internet got better once 3G—the first digital standard for cell networks—got built out around 2001. But phones didn't yet have screens that could actually display a website.

Still, the category looked real to tech giants and startups. More companies piled in. But the category still mostly attracted early adopters and business users. The Geroski line showing the value of the category crept upward slowly, as it typically does. The mass market stayed on the sidelines, curious, waiting, reading stories in the press, unsure what product to buy or whether these new things were worth the investment. As the number of players in the category rose and potential customers waited and watched, it became more and more obvious that this was a category full of potential energy ready to be unlocked by a dominant design.

The first signs of a dominant design arrived on June 29, 2007. As detailed in the earlier chapter on the category creation formula, Apple's Steve Jobs took the stage that day and told us why all the previous smartphones were inadequate and why they were the reason for slow adoption of the category. As noted earlier, Jobs said from the stage: "What we want to do is make a leapfrog product that is way smarter than any mobile device has ever been and is super-easy to use."

Then he showed us Apple's first iPhone. The whole face of it was a screen—better for showing websites and images. The device could make calls, send emails, take pictures, and play music. The keyboard was on the touch screen. Eventually, it was going to have apps—software that others could develop to make the iPhone do new things.

As Geroski said, it can be hard to know why a particular design wins and becomes the dominant design. Sometimes the first to create a category sets the rules so solidly that its design wins even after challengers pile in. Other times a latecomer, like Apple, studies the flaws of previous designs and usurps all the category's players by establishing a dominant design out of nowhere. Sometimes the best technology wins but sometimes it doesn't. Sometimes the best branding and marketing wins . . . and sometimes it doesn't.

In 2007, Apple already had a rabidly loyal base that got instantly activated by the iPhone unveiling. Apple had created an elegant physical form factor that was different from anything before it, and a user experience that was the most intuitive and flexible yet. A year later, the debut of the App Store accelerated the iPhone's drive toward the dominant design. For the first time, developers anywhere could build and sell software for a phone, creating a supporting ecosystem and the sense that this phone would be able to do anything. (The early iPhone ads teed up various daily problems to solve and declared, "There's an app for that!") It all came together in a way that made the broader market begin to think, Oh, that's what a smartphone should be.

Just about one year after the iPhone's debut, Google (now Alphabet) introduced the Android smartphone operating system. It was, and still is, a near replica of the iPhone's user interface, which only reinforced that Apple had in fact created the dominant design. Over the next few years, as Apple built on the iPhone design, any device that was not on board with the dominant design seemed more and more irrelevant. As popular as the BlackBerry and its tiny keyboard had been among businesspeople, it missed out on the dominant design. Brands like Nokia and Motorola—also late to give up on their designs and adopt the dominant design—lost market share. By the late 2010s, anyone who wanted a smartphone had two choices: Apple or its copycat, Android. Pick up any smartphone today, and you will see the dominant design.

As Geroski would have predicted, once the dominant design was chosen, the number of vendors dropped, ultimately getting down to two that mattered. At the same time, the value of the category soared as the mass market got comfortable with the dominant design and adopted smartphones. The smartphone market in 2007 was $122 million. By 2010, it had more than doubled. In another two years, it more than doubled again. In 2014 the smartphone market was more than ten times larger than on the day Jobs introduced the iPhone.[4]

Apple in early 2025 was worth $3.7 trillion. The vast majority of its profits still run through the iPhone. BlackBerry got out of the device business, and in early 2025 was a software company worth $2.4 billion. That comparison shows the power of winning the dominant design—and the consequence of losing it.

White Claw Hard Seltzer and the Dominant Design

Apple won the dominant design by developing a new and different kind of system for a smartphone (physical design plus user experience plus app ecosystem), building on it year after year, and leveraging the company's loyal following to jump-start its position in the category.

But, as Geroski showed, there are many different ways a dominant design gets established. Here's another one, as illustrated by a story we referenced earlier in the book: how White Claw won the category of hard seltzer.

A Vancouver company, Mark Anthony Group, was originally founded by Anthony von Mandl to sell imported wines.

In 1996, the company introduced its own drink, Mike's Hard Lemonade—essentially carbonated vodka and lemonade in a can. The quirky drink won a following among young people. It wasn't until twenty years later, in 2016, that Mark Anthony Group introduced another new alcoholic beverage: a light, flavored alcoholic seltzer in a can called White Claw.

By then, social media had arisen as a marketing force, driven largely by independent influencers. Millennials started posting testimonials and funny bits about White Claw, creating a hashtag, #ClawLife. A few other niche hard seltzers had been around for a few years before White Claw, but none got such traction on social sites, and hard seltzer in general remained a tiny category among alcoholic beverages.

The dominant design moment happened in 2019, around six years after the category was born. A YouTube comedian, Trevor Wallace, made a video in which he proclaimed a "White Claw summer" and used the phrase "Ain't no laws when you're drinking Claws." The original video quickly racked up several million views. Suddenly, a young audience seemed to wake up to hard seltzer and focused on White Claw as the category leader. Sales of White Claw quadrupled from $155 million in 2018 to $627 million in 2019, according to Bloomberg. Mark Anthony Group had to race to build up production capacity.[5]

Today, White Claw leads a booming $5 billion category, maintaining about a 58 percent share of the market, according to NielsenIQ data.

A decade before, grocery stores didn't devote any shelf space to hard seltzer. Now, most stores have cleared out a section that used to be for beer and are selling numerous hard seltzer brands—a tangible sign of the arrival of a new category. In fact, beer companies from AB InBev to Pabst Blue Ribbon have launched hard seltzer brands. Yet none have been able to unseat White Claw. Once a product wins the dominant design of a category, it's very difficult to dislodge its leadership position.

Of course, Mark Anthony Group couldn't have planned to win the category this way. A series of events it didn't control contributed to White Claw becoming dominant in hard seltzers. But any company that believes it has a winnable category must be ready for the moment the dominant design gets chosen—however it may happen.

The key is to always drive to become the dominant design, recognize the moment it happens, and capitalize on it to secure the category for the long run.

Set the Rules so You Win the Dominant Design

And yet, the inherent dilemma goes something like this: Winning the dominant design is critical to winning a market category . . . and yet Geroski could not identify a common strategy for winning the dominant design.

Ultimately, strategic category design is a way to improve a company's odds of winning the dominant design. If you do everything you can to design not just your product but the category itself, and design the category in a way that favors your product over those of other entrants, you stand a better chance of influencing and, in time, owning the dominant design.

All the tactics that make up strategic category design contribute to influencing and winning the dominant design. But one in particular is targeted straight at that goal. We call it setting the category rules.

A company that successfully sets the rules for a market category retains a long-term advantage. Contenders that come into the category are forced to play by the rule setter's rules. If they don't, they'll run afoul of customer expectations. But a company has to be intentional about it. Just letting the rules happen means you may not stay in control of the rules, and so you'll lose one of the key levers that can help you win a category's dominant design.

What does setting the rules mean? Uber gave us a terrific example.

Every entrepreneur should flip through Uber's very first pitch deck, presented to investors in 2008—the year after Apple introduced its iPhone. (That pitch resulted in a $200,000 seed-stage investment. By the time Uber went public, it had raised a total of $24.7 billion in twenty-five rounds of funding.)

Uber's deck started out much as we advise any company to begin its pitch: by laying out the problem to be solved. Basically, the problem in 2008 was that taxis suck and taxi monopolies control the market.

Beginning at the deck's fifth slide, Uber presented the rules for this never-before-seen category of transportation service. Those rules included: You have to be a member to use the service; a mobile app matches a client and driver; the app shows how long you'll have to wait for a ride; and the service is prepaid cashless billing so you don't have to pay on the spot.[6]

Then on slides 9 and 16 in the original Uber deck (as seen above), the founders rolled out what was probably the most interesting rule for the category. Slide 9 showed an integration with Google Maps. And slide 16 was a category design thing of beauty. It said: "Cars hover in statistically optimized positions." And it showed a map of where cars should be.

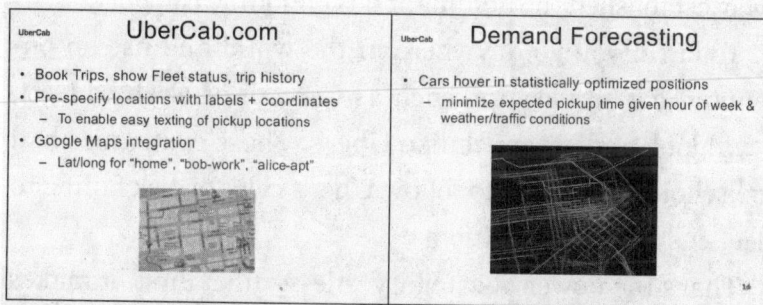

UberCab.com	Demand Forecasting

• Book Trips, show Fleet status, trip history
• Pre-specify locations with labels + coordinates
  – To enable easy texting of pickup locations
• Google Maps integration
  – Lat/long for "home", "bob-work", "alice-apt"
	• Cars hover in statistically optimized positions
	  – minimize expected pickup time given hour of week & weather/traffic conditions

If you think about it, in 2008, when only a small percentage of people had iPhones, a ride-hailing app could've ended up looking and acting in any of dozens of different ways. Uber's design was not obvious or predestined. But Uber's founders thought a ridesharing service should have an app that would show cars on a map, find a ride with a click, and have the ride prepaid through your credit card. Uber laid out all those rules during its first attempt at raising funding.

The rules have since been an enormous factor in Uber's dominance of its category. Uber officially opened for business in 2009. By the time Lyft came along in 2012, the market category of ridesharing had momentum, and customer expectations had been set by Uber.

If you remember, when Lyft—originally Zimride—first started, it tried to differentiate itself from Uber by emphasizing that rides were a fun social thing (you'd meet new people sharing rides!) and made drivers affix a pink mustache to the front of their cars. Before long, Lyft had to abandon those elements and play by Uber's rules because that's what customers expected. Lyft had no choice but to make its service and its app look and act much like Uber's. Uber's early rules effectively established the dominant design for the category.

Today, if you go anywhere in the world and use an on-demand car service app such as Careem or Grab or Gett, it will look and act much like Uber's. Those companies had little choice. They had to follow Uber's rules or risk failing to meet customer expectations.

That's the power of category rule-setting. First, it makes everyone else look like a follower. Second . . . the rule setter stays in charge of the rules. As technology and the market change, the rule setter can update the rules, and then the other players have to follow.

How do you become the rule setter? For starters, you can't set the rules if someone else is already the category's rule setter. To put it another way, it's almost impossible to go into an established category that has an established category leader and dominant design, and take over the rules.

One way to become a rule setter is by establishing a new market category. If you're creating something that didn't exist before—as Uber did—you have a blank canvas. There are no rules yet, so you can set them.

The other way is to come into an emerging, still-chaotic category where no one has effectively standardized the rules, and take over the rules, as Apple did.

Uber and Apple were intentional about the rules. They were there in Uber's first pitch deck. They were laid out by Steve Jobs at the iPhone's unveiling. A company's leadership team should discuss the rules and write them down so everyone in the company understands them. The way we do that in strategic category design is in the POV. The goal of the POV is to clearly articulate why the category needs to exist and what it should look like, and part of describing what it should look like is describing how the product or service should work—i.e., the rules.

All of which helps set rule-setting in motion for the company. Give the POV to the product team, and it can understand what to build, and in the process of building the product, the team will solidify and deepen the rules. The POV and product will inform sales and marketing on how to talk about the product, and as they spread the message, they are telling the customer base about the rules.

In time, users come to believe a product in this new category must work in a certain way—the way the rule setter makes it work. Then it becomes hard for anyone else to come into the category and play by different rules.

The ability to set the rules of a new category is the ultimate power play in business. If you're not writing the rules, you're playing by someone else's rules.

So the question is: Do you want to be a rule follower, or do you want to set the rules for everyone else?

How the Category Cycle Informs Strategy

For an entrepreneur or leadership team, Geroski's work can help inform strategy.

Put Geroski's category life cycle graphic up on a screen or on the wall. Whatever category you think you're in, try to understand where in the life cycle you are now. Is it the category's day one, and you are creating it and are the only one in it? Is it years into the life of the category, but no one has yet won the dominant design? Or has the dominant design been established, and the category is in the process of shedding competitors while growing the market?

If the category is just beginning, you have an opportunity to set the rules. If the category matters, expect competitors to rush in with different designs and rules. If competitors emerge, that helps validate the category, but then your job is to keep control of the rules and ultimately win the dominant design.

If the category is still developing, you still have a chance of establishing the rules and winning the dominant design, but you'll have to study why no design has caught on, and offer a design and rules that beat all the others. You'll know you're successful if you see a surge in adoption and a winnowing of competitors.

If a category is mature, don't bother trying to set rules

or win the dominant design. If you really want to be in that category, you'll have to get on board with the established dominant design and try to carve out a few points of market share by competing on features or price.

Or, just avoid a mature category, and instead look for a way to do something different that looks and feels like a new category, and start the category evolution cycle all over again.

Often a mature older category gets usurped by a new category, the way smartphones displaced analog cell phones, or streaming TV has been displacing cable TV. Companies often have a hard time leaping from an old category they dominated to a new one they don't, which is why tech giants rarely hold on to their power positions generation after generation. IBM couldn't be beat in mainframe computers. Instead, it got diminished by a new category of personal computers. At some point, a new category will challenge Facebook, Google, Amazon, and Apple. But no one is likely to unseat them inside the categories they dominate.[7]

Geroski told us there is no way to absolutely ensure your design will win, just as there's never been a sure way to know a song will be a top-ten hit. Still, understanding that the ultimate goal is to win the dominant design in a flourishing new category can inform a company's strategy and focus its efforts. Staple Geroski's chart to the wall, and work to be the dominant company when the category's value hits its peak.

7

Superhero POVs

Many business leaders believe that once they prove their product is better, people will buy it. Show investors impressive numbers and the company will get funding. Grow earnings and the stock will rise.

But science says that's not the way things always work. As rational as we like to think we are, people tend to make decisions to buy or invest based on emotions and cognitive biases, not logic or data. And their emotions are often driven and manipulated by stories, which might come to them through the media, in a speech, at a meeting, or from friends, social network posts, or any number of sources.

So if that's true, then one of the most important jobs for a CEO or entrepreneur is to create and spread a story that effectively influences emotions to help the business. That's arguably as vital a use of a leader's energy as managing finances or improving the product.

In strategic category design, such a story is what we call a point of view, or POV.

Sound irrational? Well, consider research by Taly Reich of the Yale School of Management and Sam Maglio of the University of Toronto. They conducted a rigorous behavioral study to try to understand whether the way people make a decision influences how strongly they stick to that decision, as opposed to later changing their minds. The researchers set up an experiment that forced one group of people to make a decision based on facts and rationality, and another group to base their decision on their emotions.[1] Time after time, the researchers found that those who decided based on emotions defended their decision and stuck to it, even when presented with competing facts. Those who decided rationally could be moved to change their minds.

"The unique thing about our paper is that we look at the post-choice phase: sure, we make a choice, but then we're exposed to all this new information, to other options that can threaten the choice we made. How do we protect our choices in the face of that?" Reich told *Yale Insights*. "What we document is a basic effect where deciding based on feelings seems to offer people more choice protection," Reich said.[2]

Think of Microsoft's commercials in 2010 telling you that Bing produced better search results than Google. By then, the majority of people had emotionally bought into Google and felt comfortable with it. Microsoft's facts meant little to the market—and couldn't budge Google's market share.

Yale is also the home base for Robert Shiller, a Nobel laureate who predicted the 2008 housing crisis and made behavioral economics a significant field of research. In 2019, Shiller published his book *Narrative Economics: How Stories Go Viral & Drive Major Economic Events.* Shiller argues in the book that economists who just study the numbers miss the most powerful drivers of historical economic trends. He bounces through time to show how popular narratives influenced people to make irrational but emotional decisions that had enormous economic impact.

Financial bubbles are an example. Popular narratives in the mid-2000s about how housing prices would always rise, mixed in with the story that the American dream involved owning real estate, were actually unsubstantiated myths. But the stories struck emotional chords and people made irrational decisions that they wholeheartedly believed were right. The stories won; the facts lost. Millions of people wound up financially devastated in 2008 when the value of their homes collapsed.

During the dot-com boom of the late 1990s, Shiller notes, Silicon Valley proffered a myth that the embryonic internet "changes everything"—including age-old concepts of profitability and sound management. Millions of people bought the story, confidently invested in dot-com companies at crazy valuations, and lost their shirts when the facts finally proved the myth wrong and the industry nearly collapsed after 2000. "Ultimately, the mass of people whose decisions cause economic fluctuations aren't very well-informed . . .

and yet their decisions drive aggregate economic activity," Shiller writes. "It must be the case that attention-getting narratives drive those decisions."[3]

A company's POV is that kind of attention-getting narrative. It's meant to have a compelling arc and hit emotional notes. Its goal is to make people feel that a category of product or service that doesn't yet exist really *must* exist, and that the company presenting the POV knows how to make it exist.

An effective POV hits on an emotional level first, giving you—the company's leaders—an opening to later present the facts that seal the deal.

We've worked on strategic category design with hundreds of startup CEOs. These are all supersmart people. When they talk about their company or product, most tend to favor logic and numbers. Technical founders, especially, are rightfully proud of what they've built, so they want to tell you what their product does and how it works.

All of which is aimed at the rational parts of the brains of potential investors, customers, or hires. But if a company doesn't influence emotions and biases first, all the facts and product specs it can muster won't move the needle.

There's the famous story about how Steve Jobs persuaded John Sculley to leave his position as president of PepsiCo to join Apple in the 1980s. Jobs didn't win Sculley over by showing him Apple's finances or product road map. One emotional appeal got Sculley on board: "Do you want to sell sugar water for the rest of your life, or do you want to change the world?"

Think, too, about most pharmaceutical ads you see. They start with the way some condition negatively impacts your life, then shows a happy life once you use that drug. It's purely emotional. Drug ads don't delve into how the drug works—no details about how it blocks some kind of protein or opens up capillaries.

One of the often-cited explanations of how and why this approach works comes from New York University psychologist Jonathan Haidt. In his book *The Happiness Hypothesis: Finding Modern Truth in Ancient Wisdom*, Haidt compared our decision-making process to a rider on an elephant.

The rider is the rational part of our brains. It deals in facts and reason. It makes plans, does the math, plots the course.

The elephant is everything else that's going on in our brains. Or, as Haidt put it in a podcast discussion, the elephant represents "99 percent of what's going on in your mind that you're not aware of." These are the cognitive biases that have been embedded there. These are our emotions and fears and needs.[4]

The elephant is far bigger and more powerful than the rider, Haidt explained. If the elephant doesn't want to move or change direction, the rider can't make it. If the elephant gets touched off by something and wants to charge in the wrong direction, the rider doesn't have much chance of stopping it.

Yet if the elephant is on board, the rider can easily guide it. They can work in sync.

Haidt uses this metaphor to make a point: If you want

to persuade someone, reach the elephant first. Once you get the elephant's attention, then appeal to the rider with logic and facts.

On the other hand, if you begin by addressing the rider but don't appeal to the elephant—i.e., emotions—you're wasting your time. The rider won't get the elephant to budge. It's also important to address both elephant and rider, not just one of them—but always the elephant first.

With that in mind, try looking at a bunch of tech company websites. You'll likely find that almost all of them begin by telling you what the company does. They probably cite some statistics and throw around impressive-sounding technical terms for good measure.

All that is directed at the rider. Rarely do you find a tech company that first appeals to the elephant with a pitch aimed at emotions.

When working with companies on strategic category design, we try to find a way to appeal to the elephant first. When we write a company's POV, we use numbers and product specs sparingly and strategically. We want to describe the problem that potential customers are grappling with: the problem the company's product will help alleviate.

We want the elephant—the customer's emotions—to feel that the company understands its fears and needs. By being empathetic, the company builds emotional trust. The elephant thinks: If you understand my problem, maybe you also understand how to fix it.

Once the elephant gets on board, then facts and logic can help convince the rider. That's when you get into how a product works and the details of what it does. If the elephant is assuaged and the rider buys into the details, together they will move where you want them to move.

In other words, the customer will buy.

This also works when pitching investors. Most pitch decks aim at the rider first. The best ones begin by addressing the elephant. The same goes for job descriptions and recruiting pitches. How many job descriptions have you ever read that first appeal to prospects' desires and goals? Instead, they're almost always dry facts. Make your hiring pitches emotional, the way Jobs addressed Sculley.

Companies don't need category design to learn how to address the elephant. But the category design process can help. The first goal of category design is to identify a new market category that a company can create or claim. A key to winning that category is defining and describing it in a way that captures the elephant first. Figure out what the elephant needs to hear. Then articulate that in an empathetic way. That will open people's hearts so they can embrace the facts about what you do and how you do it.

Hand in hand with emotions are our cognitive biases. For insights into the way these biases work, and how to apply those insights in category design, we turned to Daniel Kahneman (who died at ninety in 2024) and especially his book *Thinking, Fast and Slow.*[5]

Knowing, per Kahneman, that biases often influence people's buying decisions more than facts, a company should try to influence those biases. The way to win a market category and lead it over time is to plant the bias in customers' minds that your product or service is the absolute best one to get . . . even if it's not the best. Such biases are why most people first think "iPhone" when they need a new smartphone, or why we reflexively buy Heinz ketchup without thinking or caring if some other ketchup may taste better.

Our brains are governed by more than fifty different cognitive biases that push us toward decisions. This actually serves as an important shortcut system—a way to make decisions faster and easier, especially when overwhelmed by too much information.

For example, one of the biases is called the anchoring effect. It's a tendency for an early bit of information to affect our view of all the information that comes after. The first offer in a negotiation has a powerful impact on offers that come after—just as the first company to describe a problem and solution wins a powerful place in the public's minds. Other companies that come into that category later get judged against that early company.

The choice supportive bias is a tendency to give positive qualities to an option we've chosen just because we've chosen it. Once a company gets customers to commit to its product in a new category, they're likely to feel certain that the product they chose is the best even if something slightly better comes along. This is a reason category winners can't easily be overcome by a competing product or service even if the competing product is better.

Groupthink bias describes a tendency to believe things because other people do. Brain studies have shown that when we hold an opinion that differs from others in a group, our brains produce an error signal, warning us that we might be wrong. In a category, customers embrace the dominating design because that's what everyone else is using.

To establish and win a new market category, you have to make your customers' brains feel emotionally safe and happy about buying from you versus anyone else. A great story is a way to get that process rolling.

A POV Guide

Here's our guide to creating an effective POV.

We'll start with some general pointers. . . .

To maximize the emotional impact, the story needs to be a story—with a beginning, a middle, a climax, and a resolution. (In less than one thousand words, because, you know . . . attention spans.)

The POV should rely on numbers sparingly—skip the total addressable market stats or growth curves. It should shy away from citing analyst reports or academic studies. Make bold statements about the way things are: "62 percent of workers surveyed expressed dissatisfaction with their present positions" has less gut impact than "Most people hate their jobs."

A POV is not a marketing pitch for your product. Its purpose is to clearly and emotionally define the problem and the solution to the problem.

A good POV is aimed at convincing us that toothpaste will keep our teeth from rotting, not at selling the properties of Crest. A POV's goal is to create a space in people's minds for a new category that your product can fulfill. Create demand so you can supply the answer.

Refer to your company and product sparingly, and only toward the end of the POV, after you've described the problem and introduced the solution. If you find yourself ticking off product features, pull back and ask whether that's really the category (toothpaste) or your twist on the solution (nice minty flavor).

All in all, write in a way that's similar to a TED Talk, with simple, straightforward sentences. We like to say that a great POV is kind of a business poem.

Give it the "barstool test." The story and language should be straightforward enough so that you could read it to any intelligent person you meet at a bar, and they'd understand it. That means staying away from industry jargon, acronyms, and mushy marketing-speak.

Make your audience want more—not hope you'll shut up. A POV is not designed to say everything you want to say.

The POV is key to everything that follows. Once a company gets its narrative right, it can tell that story to all of its employees to get their buy-in. It can tell a version to investors to get funding. The marketers can create a version of the story to lure customers. Once the product team embraces the story, the engineers and designers will deeply understand what the product should do.

And at IPO time, the story becomes the stock's story—and stocks with a story often perform better than the rest because they play to our emotions and biases.

The Plot of a POV (and Yes, It Needs a Plot)

There may be many different ways to write and structure a POV. We've landed on one that works and is easy for others to adopt—because it's based on the kind of story arc that humans have used for thousands of years.

It also happens to be the plot structure of most superhero movies.

For example, the beginning of a Batman movie is usually focused on the villain. The Joker comes to town and is causing mayhem. The movie makes us really wallow in how bad the problem is—we see the Joker blowing things up, killing people, threatening the whole city or world.

There's a point in the movie where mere humans try all sorts of things to stop the villain. The police fail. The army fails. No conventional means of battling the Joker work.

So it's time for a different solution. We get introduced to Batman. He is the solution. But first we have to know a little about Batman—his powers and why he is capable of solving the Joker problem in a way that no one else has tried.

Once we understand Batman, the movie shows us the solution in action. We see Batman battle the Joker. There may be ups and downs, but as the story unfolds, we come to see why Batman will ultimately win.

Once Batman wins, there are always some final scenes of life after the problem has been solved. People are safe and happy.

A powerful category-defining POV follows a similar arc.

It begins with the problem and wallows in it. You want your audience to feel how frustrating or even dangerous this problem is. You want your audience to know that you know the pain they feel.

Then show why conventional means of solving this problem fail. Tell us why the problem persists despite alleged solutions that have been around for ages. Denigrate and deposition status quo solutions as failures.

Then introduce your Batman. Your Batman is the category—a new and different solution to the problem. Tell us something about the superpowers of this solution. Tell us why it is uniquely able to defeat the problem while so many other solutions have failed.

Show us the solution in action—how this new category of solution works and its impact on the problem. Anyone who reads it should be convinced that this is how the problem should be solved, no matter what company develops it. This section of the POV is an important part of setting the rules, as described earlier.

And once the new solution wins, tell us how good everything is afterward. Paint a picture of what's possible once the problem is defeated.

Finally, use the last few lines to tell us why your company is best positioned to provide the solution—in other words, why your company will create and win the category. This part doesn't need to be long. You've established that the category must exist and what its rules are, so at the end you just have to sign off by putting your brand on the category.

Follow that structure, and you'll cast the category that

you're creating as a superhero to anyone who suffers from the problem.

An Example: Chrysler's Imagined 1980s Minivan POV

It's not really kosher for us to share an actual client's POV, so instead we created an imagined POV for a category developed long ago: the minivan.

We tried to consider how Chrysler, as it set out to create the minivan category in the 1980s, might have written its POV.

We've included instructive italicized notes throughout. Also, keep in mind that this POV is set in the 1980s, when gas prices were a major issue, baby boomers were having kids and moving to the suburbs, and electric cars were nonexistent.

Chrysler's POV for the Minivan Category

Note: The first 40 percent is what we call the dark side—all about the problem. Stay focused on the problem. Don't veer into the solution.

As a modern 1980s family, you're always on the road—driving the kids to school and sports, going on road trips to see relatives, running out for groceries or pizza.

But for all of that, you don't have the right vehicle.

Once you got married, you probably bought a house in the suburbs and had a couple of kids—or more.

Kids come with a lot of stuff, like car seats and diaper bags. Or, when they're a little older, friends.

Note: Try to tee up the problem quickly. You want it to hit like a jab to the nose. Then throw a few more jabs.

The house you bought is probably some distance from family, which means you end up carting the kids and their stuff to see relatives—plus suitcases if the relatives are far away.

So you've got kids and stuff and have to drive a lot, but the sedan you had when you were only a married couple can't handle it.

You suddenly find you have a *family transportation gap.*

Note: Name the villain—i.e., the problem. There's no rule about when to name it—sometimes it seems to come up quickly; sometimes later in the dark side. The rest of this half of the POV digs into the problem. What causes it? What are the ramifications? Make it concrete with a few tightly worded specific examples. But keep it high-level for the most part.

The family transportation gap means siblings and friends wind up squished together in the back seat of a too-small car.

Of course, when siblings are too close together, half the time they get in fights, making you crazy as you drive.

All the stuff you have to transport can't fit in the trunk, so you have to pile some on the kids' laps.

Add a dog to the mix, and a sedan can start to feel like a jammed clown car.

Some people opt for other solutions to the family transportation gap—other vehicles that are bigger than a sedan.

Note: De-position older solutions or competition when-ever possible as having failed to solve this problem.

You can get a station wagon, but that doesn't give you much more room—it's just a stretched-out sedan.

Yes, sure, with a station wagon you can let kids ride in the open space in back—where there are no seats or seat belts. Slam on the brakes and they'll go flying.

Another solution may be a full-size van. They are much bigger. So big, in fact, that they're too tall to pull into a garage.

A van also drives like a truck and gets rotten gas mileage. These days, that's expensive.

All in all, the auto companies have failed families by only offering vehicles that are either too small to make a difference or too big to be practical.

Note: Toward the end of this half, bring up the villain again and remind people it has not been defeated.

So the family transportation gap lives on, making moving your family around challenging, if not miserable.

But that's changing.

Introducing a new category of family vehicle: the minivan.

Note: This is the turnaround from the dark side to the light side. We introduce and name the category: i.e., the hero of this story. Right after introducing the category, write one or two paragraphs that are the boilerplate version of what the category is.

The minivan is a new-era family vehicle that drives like a car, fits in a garage, and has the kind of expanded room today's families need.

It doesn't just shrink the van or expand the car, but is a whole new concept for family transportation.

A minivan is built for comfort, has seating capacity for seven and room for everyone's luggage, yet is a relative miser on gas.

Minivans finally solve the family transportation gap. With your kids in the captain's chairs in back, they won't even be close enough to fight.

Note: Try to bring back a mention of the villain and remind people the category vanquishes the villain. The rest of this half unpacks the category and how it works, starting with the big picture and then unfolding important details. This is where you're setting the rules for the category so everyone else has to follow them. Note that all other makes of minivans after Chrysler's have most of the same characteristics.

The first minivans have a longer wheelbase than cars and double the cargo space of a typical station wagon. They come with a liftgate rear door for easy loading, like those on a station wagon.

In the front are two bucket seats, comfortable for long drives. Under the passenger seat is a storage drawer more than twice as big as a standard glove compartment. The next row has two captain's chairs, separated by a space between them.

A third row is a bench seat that seats three and folds down for extra cargo space.

Minivans are the first autos in the world with cup holders. No more drinks tipping over on a sharp turn.

And minivans are built on a carlike chassis, with smooth

suspension, power steering, and disc brakes. They're as easy to drive as any sedan.

Note: After describing the category solution that lands in the adjacent possible, throw in a little vision—where this category is heading in the future. Make people feel like you know where the journey goes.

Over time, minivans will have more options, including high-end sound systems with cassette decks, leather seats, and variable seat configurations.

Extended wheel-length versions will allow a family that has two kids today to buy a larger model when the third or fourth kid comes along.

At some point, minivans will be available in an electric version. If gas prices keep rising at the rate they have in recent years, electric vehicles will become a godsend.

Note: The last 10–20 percent: Introduce the company and its version of the solution. You shouldn't have to explain too much—the category story above does most of that work. This is the first place where you use your brand.

At Chrysler, we've built the first minivans.

Ours are called the Dodge Caravan and Plymouth Voyager.

Both models drive like a car and fit in a garage. They have the space and configurations to easily move around any size family.

Both the Caravan and Voyager come with cup holders. Soon, we'll offer minivan seats in soft Corinthian leather.

Note: Wrap things up, and maybe bring up the villain again and add a tagline.

Our minivans finally end the family transportation gap.

We offer a solution that keeps families happy no matter how much time they spend on the road.

Chrysler: The family car company.

Writing a POV as a Team Sport

A lot of chief executive officers or chief marketing officers want to sit down, alone, and write a point of view for the company. That would be a mistake.

At the beginning of the book, we told you how we run our workshops and why we do it that way. We want the process to involve the company's most influential leaders, across disciplines. Anyone who employs strategic category design internally, on their own, should want that, too.

The team discussion brings in new ideas and challenges old ones. It creates a sense of unity—that we're all in this together. The work of writing, discussing, and refining the POV helps the team feel a part of the outcome. Everyone feels aligned. They come out of the workshop ready to evangelize the POV to their internal teams, and then out to the market.

If you're the CEO, you don't want your team to feel like you handed down a POV and told them to follow it. If you're a CMO, you don't want the rest of the company to feel like you wrote something for the marketing team, and everyone else can ignore it. To be effective, a POV needs the support of every leader in the company.

So a good way to successfully create a POV at your

company is to go through a version of the steps we outlined in chapter one.

First day: Organize an all-day meeting with your leadership team. One or two people need to facilitate the discussion. Rely on the category formula, the adjacent possible, and the Geroski graph to help drive the conversation. Get everyone's views. Debate. Keep this going until, by the end of the day, there is at least some consensus around the context, the missing, and the innovation needed to develop a category-defining POV. Everyone at this point should "see" the category.

Resist the temptation to do this in a couple of hours or to spread the conversation out over days or weeks. As we said earlier, momentum and intensity matter. One day, one discussion, make it count.

Middle days: First of all, pick one person to be the writer. Group writing is like group cooking—you'll end up with a bland stew. The writer's task is not to create a finished, polished POV. The task is to write a version of the POV that captures what the room discussed, knowing it will drive further discussion and revisions.

For the writer: Write more, then distill. Making it shorter will force simplicity. Edit hard. Then edit hard again. Finally, read it aloud. If it sounds clunky when you say it, then fix it and edit some more.

Try to find a balance between leaning too far into the future or too close to the status quo. It is important to keep the adjacent possible in mind.

Consider leaving the category name blank while you write

the first draft. Then, when the story takes shape, the category name may become obvious. The category name should be two or three words, utilitarian, and not feel like a brand name. It's the *category* name, like microwave oven or customer relationship management. If you can't come up with a good name, consider leaving that part blank and discussing it with the team later. (More on category naming coming up.)

At CDA, we take two days to develop and write a draft POV. But we've been doing that for years and two days is usually enough. Yet that may not be the case for everyone. It's OK if it takes three days, or a week. However, be mindful of momentum and intensity. We believe it's better to get the POV draft written within a week, with the second workshop for the POV discussion taking place no more than a week after the initial session.

Once you (the writer) are happy with the POV, put it all on slides, one or two sentences per slide. Just the words—no need for graphics. You want to be able to present the POV back to the team slide by slide, so every sentence and word gets attention.

Final day: Again, schedule a whole day with the exact same team that was in the room on day one. Have the writer read the POV aloud, projecting it slide by slide so the room hears it and reads it.

When finished, have a general discussion about the POV. Is it directionally right? What did it get right or wrong? How did it feel? Is the concept right even if some words and details need to be fixed? Keep it high-level for now. Get every person's input around the table.

Pause. Take a breath. Read it through entirely again. Give everyone a chance to comment.

Then start at the first slide, read it, and talk about it. Don't try to edit live, as a group. That can be chaotic. Instead, take notes about the comments. Do this for every slide of the POV.

If the POV is close, just needing minor edits, take a break after gathering all the comments for all of the POV. Have the writer go somewhere quiet and clean up the POV on the slides. Bring everyone back to the room and do another read-through. Discuss again. Make small tweaks as you go. Repeat as necessary. Don't give up until the team has a POV they can all rally around.

By the end of the day, the POV should be set. Everyone should feel like they'd sign their name to it.

Once everyone agrees on the POV, lock it down! No tinkering after the fact. (Once the Declaration of Independence was signed, Thomas Jefferson didn't go back and change a few words.)

Put the POV into a form that can be read and shared by the team that helped create it. Everyone should feel like it describes the company's future.

How to Name a Category

A vital part of defining a category is giving it a name.

Merriam-Webster's Collegiate Dictionary's definition of *innovation* is "a new idea, method, or device." And a new market category is essentially an innovation that the world needs. (There are lots of innovations that the world doesn't need. For instance: quadraphonic stereos and inside-the-egg scramblers. Or, as noted earlier, Segways. They don't end up creating flourishing market categories.)

In the room with our clients, the naming part always seems to stir the biggest debate. We may perfectly nail the POV narrative, but still struggle with the two or three words that name the category.

It can be tricky. A category name should be descriptive, understandable, and neutral enough so it is a category and not a brand. You want competitors to be able to adopt it, too—a category isn't a *category* if it only has one player.

The name can't sound too strange or futuristic—the market might not get it. Yet it shouldn't sound like meaningless jargon or like something that's already been around. It has to have some freshness to it: understandable yet intriguing. It should feel like it's leading us somewhere new.

Some examples of category names you would know: *cloud computing, search engine, minivan, hard seltzer,* and *microwave oven.* While they once described something new, by now they are part of the vernacular. That's a sign of a good name.

There are a lot of ways to land on a good category name. Sometimes the category POV leads to an obvious name—those are the easy ones. Other times, we've gotten into lengthy brainstorming sessions, listing words and concepts and trying to find a combination that the room can embrace.

We've found one way to think about category names that's a little more methodical and backed up by academic research. It was inspired by a 2021 article by two Yale professors, Jerker Denrell and Balázs Kovács, titled "The Ecology of Management Concepts." This study looked at why certain new ideas catch on and become popular.[6]

One of their conclusions has implications for category naming. As the professors described, as noted in an article by Dylan Walsh: "Popular ideas often ride the coattails of other popular ideas. They also tend to be composed of like elements. If a concept is new or unknown or both, then we find it benefits by appearing together with other famous concepts, and by covering similar ground."

In other words: Snap a new-sounding word onto a familiar-sounding word.

If you think about it, innovators have been doing this for ages. It's a way to signal something new and create the feeling of forward motion—like the new thing is taking us somewhere. When gas-powered cars were first invented, they were, of course, dubbed the horseless carriage. Everyone in the late 1800s understood what a horse-pulled carriage was. A carriage that moved yet didn't need a horse? That sounded like a future they could get their heads around—in two words.

When electricity was new, the word was often used as a modifier to signal a new category. Those early contraptions that could clean dirty dishes were sold as electric dishwashers. Similarly, in that era you would find ads for electric drills, electric irons, and electric lights.

In the 1970s, the idea of a computer that an individual could own seemed bizarre—most people knew computers as big, hulking machines that buzzed in back rooms at corporations. When the category got labeled personal computers, it helped bring us all along—we understood *personal* and *computer,* but putting them together opened up new possibilities.

As PCs got popular, we started sending messages, calling them electronic mail. The term married the familiar *mail* with a word that made it new: *electronic.*

Those category names mentioned earlier—cloud computing, search engine, microwave oven—all have that same property. In the 1990s, matching *cloud* with *computing* pulled us to a new idea from an old idea. *Engine* futurized *search.* In the 1970s, not many of us knew what an actual microwave was (a tiny wave, apparently), but it sounded cool enough to futurize the big old baking ovens in our kitchens.

This labeling idea is still at work today. Artificial intelligence has been around for decades and is reasonably well understood. Once ChatGPT came along, the category needed a name that could take us from what we knew to what was coming. *Generative* got paired with *AI* and now we accept generative AI as a thing.

So with our clients, this new + old pairing can help with the naming debate. If we're stuck, we can make a two-column list. One column can be words the market already uses and understands. The other can be appropriate words that push the old concept to a new place. Before long, a pairing pops out that makes sense.

As a bonus, consultant and author Ken Rutsky points out that these kinds of new + old terms are more likely to catch on as memes. "Striking a balance between what's known and what's novel is key. This approach piques interest and curiosity, encouraging your audience to delve deeper into what your category offers," he writes in his ebook *Making #CategoryMemes Stick: How Category Memetics Can Help You Spread Your #CategoryMeme.*[7]

However, settling on a name is not the end of the story. We've always advised clients that category names evolve over time. Once a category name is released into the wild, the creator no longer controls it. That's one way it's very different from a brand. A name can help get a category off the ground, but then customers, analysts, and competitors start using it and perhaps they modify it or shorten it as the name becomes more familiar.

The Yale study understood that, too. The professors found that, at some point, the association of the new with the old becomes unnecessary. Once all dishwashers are obviously electric, why bother adding *electric* to the name? Personal computers just become computers. Microwave ovens and cloud computing went the other way. The first just became a microwave. Now, if you use AWS or Azure, you're just using the cloud.

That's how innovators take people to the future—even in the words they use. The world rarely takes great leaps into science fiction. We get pulled from the past into the future, one step and one term at a time.

CATEGORY NAMING GUIDELINES:

- Make it utilitarian, not clever. It's not your brand. It's a term you want competitors, partners, analysts, and the general public to use.

- Consider marrying a familiar word to a new-sounding modifier, like adding *cloud* to *computing* or *microwave* to *oven*.
- It should sound interesting and new, yet not so strange that it seems like sci-fi.
- Stay away from jargon. Simple and straightforward make it more memorable.
- Consider it a term that will help launch the category, but be ready for it to evolve as it gets into use. The market may shorten or adjust it. Go with the flow and embrace that.
- Make sure it's not already in use and that it doesn't invoke a meaning that may be detrimental.
- Once you nail it, make sure it stays open-source. Buy the URLs so no one else can use them to claim the category. Don't trademark the term, but file an intent-to-use (ITU) application so you can prevent others from trademarking it.

Naming a Villain and a Thing

Names are a powerful way to get into people's brains. Give something complex a sticky name, and it becomes much more memorable than all the details. It turns into a shorthand that customers, investors, or the media can refer to.

For a similar reason, we've also found that it's impactful to name the villain and to name what we call *a thing*.

Category design pushes companies to clearly and emotionally describe the problem they solve. The key is to go deep and really wallow in all the ways this problem causes pain or costs money. And then, consolidate all the points made about the problem by giving it a utilitarian yet attention-getting name.

Here's a great and utterly familiar villain name: tooth decay. Yeah, it causes all kinds of problems, from toothaches to bad breath. But it all gets summed up in a phrase we all know. For a company, the villain is what the new category of product or service defeats. Tooth decay, in this case, gets defeated by the category of product called toothpaste.

Other good villain names might include climate change, processed food, or spam (the kind in your email inbox). Some of the great classic TV commercials teed up a villain name that could be fixed by a new product. One that comes to mind were the 1970s ads that tormented people with the idea that their clothes would have "ring around the collar." The way to beat it? Wisk detergent.

We worked with the Israeli company Ripples, which makes a digitally connected machine that can download and print any kind of image on the tops of drinks such as cappuccino or beer. Ripples created a category of beverage-top (bev-top) media. The villain? The naked drink gap. (Why would anyone want to serve a naked drink when it's really an attention-getting space where a message or ad can be delivered?)

Once the villain has been named, the other item that sometimes—though not always—gets identified and named is *a thing*.

A thing is an idea, concept, or feature that will be an integral part of the category, as defined by the rules set by the category winner. A thing is not the category itself, but something that makes the category special. For instance, when Apple set the dominant design for the smartphone category, a vital component of the category was a thing called an app store.

In our work with clients, maybe half the time an obvious thing arises from the POV sessions.

While in a category design session with software company BigPanda, we landed on a thing called Level Ø (LØ) Automation.

BigPanda makes software that automatically sorts and prioritizes the problems coming into the IT department, often at big data centers. Some of this automation has been done for years. When we worked with BigPanda, the company was taking that automation one step further: the AI-driven software could solve the simpler, less critical problems on its own.

In our workshop, we got talking about the traditional prioritization levels of IT support. They were—still are—called L1, L2, L3, and so on. The higher the level, the greater the emergency. An L1 problem may be routed to a lower-level IT tech. If that person can't fix it, it gets escalated to L2 for a more experienced pro to handle. BigPanda's new category of software was creating a new level of IT support before the old L1—a level where problems could get sorted by difficulty and a simple problem could get fixed by software without escalating it to a human IT person.

In the session, we chimed in to give it a name: LØ. That would be the new thing to make the category special. To IT people, it is instantly understandable. It gives potential customers a clear way to understand BigPanda's solution, and (like the app store) LØ can help distance BigPanda from a sea of competitors who are simply adding features to existing IT operations software. LØ is a strategic asset.

Another thing came into being as we worked with a startup called Twos. The company's founders started out by creating a robust app for, as they called it, writing things down. Most of its early customers were using it to make to-do lists. Some used it to jot down random thoughts or other bits of information they wanted to remember.

But list-making apps were not a new or exciting category. Twos wanted to elevate itself out of that categorization and develop something different. The arrival of useful AI could make that possible. Twos could offer a way to make lists that take action. You write down something you want to buy, the AI deciphers it, and pops up a link where you can buy it. Write down a movie you want to see, and it finds where it's playing or streaming and tells you. Together, we came up with a name for that thing: personal active lists, or PALs.

For Twos, the PALs concept resonated so strongly with users that it elevated Twos beyond just a cool app and into a movement advocating for a simpler, more intentional way to manage life.

Again, there's not always a thing that plays a role in every new market category. But seeing and naming a thing can be a powerful way to set the rules for a category and easily communicate what's special about it.

Put all these pieces together—a powerful, emotional POV narrative with a forward-leaning category name and maybe a sticky label for a villain and a thing—and a company has a foundation for everything else it will do. It has a story to tell itself about who we are, why we need to exist and flourish, and where we're taking our customers. It has alignment around language—the terms and phrases that can be used in every kind of company communications. It has a guide for the product team, a guide for investor pitches, and a guide for what kind of talent to attract.

A POV is so much more than a story. It's the foundation for a movement.

Ripples and Its Transformation into Bev-Top Media

We mentioned Ripples—the company that identified its villain as the naked drink gap and its category as bev-top media. The company, led by CEO Yossi Meshulam, knew it wanted to transition from just selling a machine to being a media company, but it couldn't quite piece together what that meant or how to talk about it. We took the company's leadership team through strategic category design, and once we read the POV aloud for the first time, Meshulam told us: "We had goosebumps. This is what we do and this is why [customers] need us."[8]

Several years later, that POV is still the North Star for Ripples and its product road map. As a media company, Ripples not only produces content but collects data with each drink, helping brands better engage with their customers. "Once we started to look at Ripples as a media company, our whole perspective changed," Meshulam says. "We are very disciplined about not losing ourselves to other directions. The POV aligns to our long-term vision."

Ripples' customers now include Guinness, Suntory, Nespresso, Gap, Hilton, Hard Rock Cafe, and Four Seasons. There are now thousands of Ripple machines around the world.

If not for discovering its category opportunity and articulating it through a POV, Meshulam said, "We would be struggling to find where we sit in the world. Would we be a bev-tech company? A printer? A social media tool? The POV . . . made our lives so much easier. We can easily explain who we are and the problem we solve. It resonates and works really, really well."

8

Ready, Set, Go

OK, so . . . let's say the leadership team has done the hard work of diving deeply into the problem to be solved, identifying the new category to create, naming the category and villain, and jointly writing and embracing a POV that both tells the story of the category and lays out its initial rules.

Then what do you do with that? It's not going to help the company much if you just declare victory and send the POV in an email to everyone. You have to set the category creation strategy in motion with a process called mobilization. And mobilization can be separated into three phases, which we've labeled *ready, set,* and *go.*

Ready

The *ready* phase starts with driving the POV throughout the company culture.

That's not usually too hard for an early-stage startup. If the leadership team has gone through this process together, then the company has a core team that is aligned in their belief in the POV and feels they were part of its development. In a startup with only a handful of people beyond the core team, everyone can be addressed one-on-one to bring them into the POV fold.

But for a bigger company or organization—any entity of more than a couple of dozen people—the first task after establishing the POV is to intentionally drive its adoption throughout the culture. You want to get your people excited. You want to bring them completely on board with the strategic direction the POV articulates. In fact, you want people who are not on board to get the message that they will no longer fit into the culture and should leave.

There is no single right way to drive a POV through a company culture. Every culture is different, and every leadership team will need to come up with a tactic that fits the culture. We've seen a range of tactics. One company sent the POV to all employees and initiated a contest for the most creative representation of the POV. One of those employees shot a video of himself flying upside down in a biplane while reading the POV aloud. (Note: This is not on our recommended list of ways to spread the POV!) Another employee made the POV into a song. One group of that company's employees turned the POV into a short play.

A more common tactic for a startup is to hold an all-hands town hall where the POV is presented by the CEO, who then leads an open discussion. At an even bigger company, the members of the leadership group that created the POV can fan out as missionaries, each holding a town hall with their team. (Presumably the people in the group that wrote the POV were in charge of different parts of the company—marketing, product, sales, finance, etc. That way, every part of the company gets a POV session from its leader.)

Don't forget the board and advisory board. You need to get them to buy into the POV and your category creation mission as soon as possible after locking down the POV. Call a special session if you have to. Tell them about the process you went through and who was involved. Present the POV to them on slides while reading it aloud. Lead a discussion and answer their questions. Never just send it to them in a document. And don't ever ask for comments or feedback—the document is finalized and was built with consensus of the team that did the work.

It's important that every person in the culture receives a POV download in a way that helps them get on board and get excited about this new direction. You want your people to feel like they are part of initiating and driving a movement. However that might work for your organization's culture, that's what you should do.

Once everyone in the culture understands the POV, put them to work making plans to execute on it. A good POV will fire up imaginations. Once the product team embraces the POV, its story should help them envision what the product should be like today, and how it should evolve. Have the team reinvent their product plans and road map so the product helps the company create and win the new market category.

The POV will reset the marketing team, giving them a new way to describe the company and its products and new ideas for messaging and advertising. (More detail on that in a few pages.) You want the sales team to recast its sales deck and pitch the product in a way that aligns with and draws from the POV. Human resources needs to consider whom the company needs to hire to build and win the category, and use the POV language in every job post so the right kind of people—those who believe in the mission—come aboard. Every part of the company needs to adopt the POV and build its future plans based on the category it describes.

Good, also, to get your legal team or outside lawyers involved. Does the POV describe some intellectual property (IP) that may need to be protected? Are there regulatory or other legal issues it raises? And make sure the lawyers do the ITU trademark filing for the category name, as mentioned in the previous chapter. Remember: You don't want to trademark the category name in order to protect it and prevent others from using it. ITU protection makes sure no one else can trademark the category name and prevent you from using it.

Set

Once the company and its culture are thoroughly indoctrinated into the POV and category mission, prepare to take the

POV outside the company's boundaries to your ecosystem and beyond. This is the *set* stage of mobilization.

The order in which you do this depends on the company's priorities. For some startups, the most important next step is to raise a round of funding. In that case, focus on creating a new pitch deck based on the POV and getting ready to take it to potential investors. (A guide to that is coming up.)

Other companies may need to first approach partners and suppliers with the new POV. In preparation for doing that, we advise companies to create what we call a directed POV. Remember that a category POV first addresses the audience's problem and then describes the solution. If you need to persuade a new slate of partners to join in your mission, you want to address *their* problem, which is likely a different problem from the one you framed for your primary customers. You're not deviating from the category or POV, but drawing from it to reframe the problem and solution.

For example, we had one client company that ultimately sells to consumers, so the main POV described the consumer's problem and the solution to it. But in order to pull off its mission, it needed to recruit restaurants and ghost kitchens to its category creation mission. That directed POV addressed the potential partners' problem of uneven demand and idle time in kitchens during off-hours, and showed that if those kitchens work with the company to solve the problem for consumers, they will get more predictable demand and use idle time to make food for delivery later. Another client, also consumer-facing, needed to recruit partners that sell to homeowners, such as hardware and furniture stores. That client's directed POV showed how the company could help deliver high-value homeowners to partners, improving sales for those partners.

It's crucial to actually write out this directed POV and lock it down. The process for doing so doesn't have to be as involved as when creating the original POV. You could assign one person to write the directed POV and perhaps hold a quick review meeting to make sure it hits the right target. By doing this, you know that whenever someone in the company talks to a partner or supplier, they'll tell the same story and use the same language, all reflecting the original POV and the company's category creation mission.

A good deal of the burden of rolling out a new category will fall on a company's marketers. If a company is creating a category, then by definition the product or service is something people haven't seen before. Marketing needs to come up with messaging that educates potential customers and the broader public. The messaging needs to draw from the POV so the story and language stay consistent, but it usually won't be the POV word for word. Think of the POV as source code for all the company's external messaging.

Mike has been a chief marketing officer at startups. Over the years of CDA working with clients, he's helped dozens of other CMOs get *set* to roll out the category by transforming the POV into a messaging platform. This, then, is *Mike's Step-by-Step Guide for Transitioning POV to Messaging*. It's a category design–oriented version of what any good marketer would do when creating a messaging platform. All of this should be completed before taking the category to the public.

Identify Key Messages: Extract the most compelling points from the POV that will resonate with your external audience. These key messages should highlight your category's uniqueness, its benefits, and its value proposition.

Develop Audience Personas: Understand who your audience is. Create detailed personas for your target market, including demographics, psychographics, and behavioral traits. This will help tailor your messages to speak directly to their needs and desires.

Craft a Messaging Framework: Build a structured messaging framework that includes:

- Core Message: Your category's overarching statement.
- Supporting Messages: Detailed messages that support your core message, tailored to different audience segments.
- Proof Points: Data, statistics, or any information that can substantiate your claims.

Create Consistent Themes: Ensure consistency in the themes across all communications to reinforce the category's identity. This includes visual identity, tone, and key terms used to describe your category.

Develop Content and Collateral: Based on your messaging framework, develop various types of content such as website copy, marketing materials, social media posts, and press releases. Redo the website so it reflects the POV and have it ready to go live when the company unveils its category.

Internal Alignment: Ensure all internal stakeholders understand and agree on the messaging. Consistency across all departments is crucial when launching a new category.

Test and Iterate: Before going live, test your messages with a small segment of your target audience. Gather feedback and make necessary adjustments. Important note: If a company is creating a new market category, it is seeing a missing and an innovation that most others don't yet see. Your job is to lead your audience to a new and better place, not give them what they request.

Launch and Monitor: Roll out your messaging across chosen channels. Monitor the performance and make tweaks as needed based on audience response and engagement metrics.

The *set* phase is also when some companies create a brand book. The messaging platform should be about the category and POV. A brand book is about the company's brand, tying it to the category and POV.

One of our clients, Guidewheel, developed a combination messaging platform and brand book that detailed everything from the elevator pitch to product names, an FAQ about the company's background, and a section called "Ways to Be Confident." (Includes points such as: "Clearly explain your vision for the next decade and beyond" and "Speak up and take a strong stance on issues that matter to you and your customers.") Many brand books also include guides on how to use the logo, colors that are acceptable, and a taxonomy of words to use.

We've seen a lot of creative ways companies tell the world

about the category they are creating. In this *set* stage, a number of our clients made videos about the POV. Ripples made an animated version that told the POV story almost word for word. LinkedIn's POV video featured most of the team that created the POV, each reading a line or two in front of the camera. Sprinklr featured its CEO, Ragy Thomas, in a spare setting talking on camera about the POV in his own words.[1]

A few clients set in motion the writing of a book. Not long after we worked with The Predictive Index to develop the category of talent optimization, CEO Mike Zani started a book that ended up being titled *The Science of Dream Teams: How Talent Optimization Can Drive Engagement, Productivity, and Happiness.* The book not only told the public about the company and category, but positioned Zani as the expert who knows how this category should work.[2] (When we last checked, it had a 4.5-star rating on Amazon.)

While books can be a powerful form of content, they have a downside: They take a long time (and a lot of work!) to write and get published. While you'd want to start a book in the *set* phase, there's little chance it would be ready when the company rolls out the category—unless that's not going to happen for a couple of years. So a book is more of a way to reinforce the category position than establish it.

A more immediate form of written content would be to craft an article to post on one of the blog platforms (like Medium, Substack, or LinkedIn) or attempt to get it published by a media outlet such as *Harvard Business Review, TechCrunch, Business Insider*, or *The Wall Street Journal.*

One of the most effective category-establishing blog

articles we've ever read was posted by the new-era defense company Anduril in June 2022, titled "Rebooting the Arsenal of Democracy: Anduril Mission Document." While Anduril is not a company we worked with, its post followed the POV formula perfectly. It convincingly laid out a new problem for the military that was being caused by advances in technology, detailed a solution that had to exist, and finally told us about Anduril and its mission.[3]

A summary of Anduril's POV—and its article—goes something like this:

The US defense industry is stuck in the past, building ever more expensive weapons that have ever more limited effectiveness in current and future confrontations. The incumbent defense industry is focused on making big, powerful hardware—fighter jets, ships, missiles, tanks. But software is and will be the key to winning wars and deterring enemies.

Today's defense companies build hardware and install software to control it. Anduril believes in a future where weapons start with the capabilities that software and data can enable, and hardware is built to help the software do its job. Anduril wants to be the company showing the way to an entirely new defense industry. The founders also argued that software-forward defense is a better deterrent at a lower cost, helping the government reverse the cycle of ever-increasing defense budgets.

By 2025, Anduril was one of the most successful new-era defense companies, but many other startups have entered the category, per Geroski. As of this writing, Anduril is valued at around $28 billion.

Set: An Investor Pitch Deck Guide

A lot of startups, especially in their early years, are in perpetual fundraising mode. So, often once a POV is locked down, one of the crucial next steps in the *set* process is to develop an investor pitch deck based on the POV.

As detailed at the start of chapter 2, the smartest investors first want to be introduced to a new category and be convinced of its potential to become huge. Their next decision is to try to pick which company will win that category, because the category winner will walk away with the majority of the category's economics. (An investor's nightmare is to pick the right category but the wrong company, and then watch some other investors get rich on the category.)

So with that in mind, your pitch deck should reflect a category-led strategy. Tee up the problem to be solved, the new category of product that will solve it, and then why your company is best positioned to win the category.

There are, of course, countless ways to make an investor pitch deck. But we've landed on a format that works well as a category-led pitch deck.

First, though, some general tips:

Fewer simple slides are vastly better than more and jam-packed slides. In the guide below, we describe the nature of what should be on the slides, but we're not suggesting that you crowd the slide with words and numbers. Your first slides are a way to capture attention so you can get to the details. The details, instead, belong in an appendix at the end. You don't want your audience to be reading lots of words on a slide while you're talking—you want them listening to you.

Tie every slide to your category strategy, making sure it all syncs with your POV narrative.

Part 1: Category Strategy

1. Title
Why: Establish who you are.

Content: Include your company name, logo, and possibly a tagline. A tagline should offer a glimpse of your idea in a few catchy words. Prescryptive, which is using technology to change the way prescription drugs are bought by consumers, used the tagline "Rewriting the script." If you don't have a good tagline, then just leave it off the deck. No tagline is better than a bad one.

2. Problem
Why: Category design positions the problem as a villain that your company is defeating in a novel way. This stirs urgency and shows your deep understanding of the market.

Content: Define the problem that your target market faces. Frame it as a villain and even name it (outdated process, inefficiency gap, a blind spot, etc.). Use data and narratives to show why this problem is unacceptable and can no longer be tolerated.

3. Category Formula

Why: VCs invest in market categories, and category designers invest in creating and developing them. The category formula is a simple way to break down why the category should exist: $f(Category) = Context + Missing + Innovation$.

Content: Show fulfillment of the formula. The context is how the world has changed for your target customers (thus creating a new problem) and/or how technology is changing (opening up a new way to solve a problem). The missing is the lack of a solution for an important problem. Now add the innovation that will solve the missing.

4. Rules

Why: It's not enough to just solve the problem; your solution needs to create a new standard in the industry. Set the rules and expectations for the category.

Content: As simply and clearly as possible, show how your product or service will work—not just the technology, but more importantly, how people will use it. Go back to the problem you defined and show how your features defeat that problem. Your goal is to make investors think your way is the right way to attack this category.

5. Vision

Why: Investors like to be part of a company that doesn't just build for today, but has a vision for what it can become in the years ahead.

Content: Show how you can build on success. If you get traction with your first product, how can you expand the category and take customers to a better future? This isn't about incremental features to add; it needs to be a broad vision. Show it from the customers' perspective—how it will change their lives for the better.

6. The Category POV
Why: A strong and simple story pulls the pieces together and gives investors a fresh way to see the world.

Content: Briefly revisit the story in one narrative arc: the problem that exists and needs to be solved in a new way; the ramifications of not solving the problem; what the solution looks like (the category); how that will improve people's lives or work; and why your team is the one who can do this.

Part 2: Details and Tactics

7. The Team
Why: Category-defining companies need extraordinary teams to execute big visions. Investors want to bet that this team can win the category.

Content: Position your team as uniquely qualified to build and win the new category you're creating. Passion is important, so highlight why this mission is important to the people on your team. If appropriate, include advisors, other investors, board members, or future team members who are also dedicated to your mission.

8. Business Model

Why: Investors want to know how you'll make money and get to profitability.

Content: Explain how your business model capitalizes on the growth of the category. Show key revenue drivers, unit economics, and scalability. Investors should see how category dominance translates into financial success.

9. Go-to-Market Strategy

Why: When creating a category, you're creating something new that the market may not yet understand. Investors will want to know how you'll educate the market and drive adoption.

Content: Outline how you plan to establish your category in potential customers' minds. Highlight partnerships, customer acquisition channels, community-building initiatives, and how you'll evangelize your category POV.

10. Traction and Milestones

Why: VCs respond more enthusiastically when they see evidence that the category is catching on, even with a small base, and getting market validation.

Content: Provide metrics, key achievements, and traction details. Include revenue, user growth, customer testimonials, media coverage, and partnerships—anything that will help show a positive direction.

11. Intellectual Property

Why: If you have protectable IP, you stand a better chance of beating competitors to category dominance.

Content: Describe IP protection or other innovations that will be hard to replicate. Demonstrate how there is a moat around your company that will be difficult, if not impossible, to breach.

12. The Ecosystem

Why: Building a category usually takes more than a product—it needs an ecosystem around it.

Content: Map out strategic partners, complementary solutions, and key stakeholders in the broader industry. Highlight any strategic relationships that position your company as the leader of the ecosystem.

13. Financial Projections

Why: Investors want to know your financial road map, especially in the context of category design where future potential is key.

Content: Show conservative and ambitious projections based on category growth. Include revenue forecasts, gross margin and other key financial indicators.

Part 3: Wrap Up

14. The Ask
Why: You've framed the opportunity; now show how the investment will help solidify your category position.

Content: Detail how much funding you're raising and what it will be used for (e.g., go-to-market activities, product development, category education). Show how this investment accelerates your path to category dominance. Don't mention valuation; wait till you have a viable lead investor, then negotiate it. Aim higher than you think.

15. Call to Action
Why: Reinforce the excitement and urgency to join you in creating this new category.

Content: Summarize your category-defining mission in a sentence. Include contact details and a clear call to action for investors (e.g., "Join us in shaping the future of [category name]").

16. Appendix
Why: If an investor gets this far and is still interested, this is where you can dump all the details that would have distracted them in the story above. The main portion of the pitch deck should be easy to digest. Too many details take away from that.

Content: Provide anything you think an investor might want to know more about: links to your team members' LinkedIn profiles, supporting documents, studies, presentations, product demo videos, press and media coverage, detailed financials, etc.

One last thing that founders sometimes forget: It's important to make a human connection, not just plow through slides. Before you even put up a slide, ask the investors in the room to introduce themselves; then introduce yourselves and tell the story of how you came to see your missing and innovation. Succinctly tell your origin story, then pop open that first slide.

Go

By this point, the company is *ready*—it has thoroughly embraced the POV and category creation mission. All the parts of the company are *set*—they've started building the product the POV describes, created marketing messages and strategies, reworked the website, dealt with legal questions, and created new sales and investor decks.

It's time to take your mission to the world—the phase we call *go*.

How each company carries out its *go* phase will be particular to that company. A *go* plan first depends on the audience you're trying to reach. A tactic to reach consumers would be very different from a tactic to reach corporate chief technology officers. A *go* plan depends on the size of your team and budget—a small startup would be hard-pressed to pull off the kind of huge, multifaceted campaign that a large, established company could plan and execute.

The book *Play Bigger* relies heavily on the idea of "lightning strikes," described as concentrating all the company's energy on one, focused, attention-grabbing splash.[4] We can't argue with the effectiveness of a great lightning strike. But we've since come to realize that it should be paired with what we call heartbeats—a constant rhythm of published content, marketing messages, announcements and events.

Most importantly for any company: Have a well-thought-out plan that involves the whole company and synchronizes with the POV. Make sure every part of the company is at the table.

If you're going to pull off a lightning strike, you want the combined force of, say, a product announcement, a brand unveiling, a funding announcement, and a social media campaign all on the same day or at the same event. Then, every unit should participate in the heartbeats. Those can include product feature updates, new hires to the leadership team, educational content about the category, celebratory announcements about milestones reached, and on and on.

It's the combination of a lightning strike (Now we've got your attention!) and the heartbeats (Now we're busy developing and winning this category!) that is so effective at driving the category message into the minds of a target audience.

In our work with companies on strategic category design, one stands out for its lightning strike and heartbeat campaign: LinkedIn Sales Solutions. Of course, we realize that not every company has the resources of a billion-dollar division of a multibillion-dollar company that's owned by a trillion-dollar company. Still, we present this as inspiration. A small startup can steal ideas from LinkedIn's campaign.

We wrote earlier in the book about LSS, which offers a version of LinkedIn tailored to sales professionals. The category design process led LSS's leaders to create a category called deep sales. The villain in that POV was shallow sales—defined as using technology to spray out uninformed and disconnected messages to as many potential customers as possible, hoping a few will bite. Too many sales teams were getting stuck in a rut of shallow sales, and it had become ineffective. In fact, that kind of selling was mostly annoying potential customers who really didn't want to see sales pitches from people they didn't know. Deep sales is a way to solve this. It builds on LinkedIn's database of opted-in professionals to help sales teams deeply understand and get to know potential customers so the sales teams can sell in a more personal way.

Once the team locked down the deep sales POV, the product team went to work making sure that what LinkedIn would offer would live up to the POV's promise. While the product team did its work, the other parts of the LSS business unit made their plans for a lightning strike and heartbeats.

Of course, deep sales is a category, not a brand. LinkedIn's job with its strike was to explain to people the problem that exists in sales so that no one can unsee it, and show why a new kind of solution—deep sales—is needed, whether LinkedIn builds it or not. But LinkedIn also wanted to establish that it understood the problem better than anyone and knew how to solve it better than anyone. That was going to take more than just an ad campaign.

As happens in a great lightning strike, LinkedIn focused its energy and resources on a concentrated effort to make its audience take notice of the new category. On the lightning strike day, the company bought a glossy ad that wrapped around the whole front of that day's *Wall Street Journal*. The wrap showcased LSS's deep sales ad campaign, which drew a contrast between shallow selling and deep selling.

That same morning, LSS took over the Nasdaq electronic billboard in New York's Times Square, again flashing the ads touting deep sales. About forty people from LinkedIn's New York office came to celebrate underneath the billboard as the images went live soon after 10 a.m. on a Tuesday. They took group pictures with the billboard overhead, which many in the group posted all over social media.

The same day, on the West Coast of the US, LSS rolled out a huge presence at Dreamforce, the annual Salesforce convention that draws 170,000 participants. LinkedIn set up a studio and café on the campus and hosted a number of live and streamed sessions, including one called "Are You Stuck in the Shallow (Selling)?"

As this was happening, dozens of LSS people from all over the world posted stories and photos on the LinkedIn platform under the hashtag #deepsales, many holding up the *Wall Street Journal* ad. LSS counted more than one thousand posts with the #deepsales hashtag over a three-day period after the launch. The deep sales explainer video described earlier, featuring the core LSS team reciting the POV, went live on social media.

As a kind of capstone, the *Harvard Business Review* published an article by Alyssa Merwin, global VP of sales for LSS, titled "B2B Selling Is in Trouble. Deep Sales Is the Answer." That was a way for LSS to make a more detailed and weighty argument for the category.

All that was the lightning strike. Then came the heartbeats.

The posts on the LinkedIn site just kept coming, over and over, day after day. The momentum of deep sales swept up LinkedIn employees all over the world, and they piled on, making #deepsales almost impossible to miss for anyone who went on the site. LSS leaders traveled around the world hosting seminars on deep sales, always posting about the events on social sites. They hosted dinners with field marketing teams to spread the POV's message and stoke momentum internally.

In early 2023, LSS delivered its new product, dubbed Relationship Explorer, unveiling it at the Salesforce World Tour event in Sydney, Australia, and promoting it in another *WSJ* full-page ad.

The LSS marketing team sent kits to more than a thousand LSS employees so they'd have material and talking points that could help them spread the POV's message. Top members of the team that created the POV fanned out to be interviewed on podcasts about deep sales.

Gail Moody-Byrd, the LSS marketing VP who drove much of the lightning strike and heartbeat planning, wrote a comprehensive post on LinkedIn about the deep sales campaign. She noted: "Our on-platform click-through and engagement rates exceeded benchmarks by 3-4 times. With our second strike, we saw even more momentum across nearly every social metric, with an engagement rate that was 10 pts higher than our benchmark. . . . With these tremendous efforts, we were able to influence hundreds of millions of potential deals through our #deepsales online and offline/in-real-life efforts."[5]

Gail concluded with some advice. She wrote:

The Keys to Success Were:
1. **Moments:** Picking a single day within the quarter for focused effort, unifying the assets with a singular hashtag.
2. **Content:** Creating powerful content and planning for its publication via a time-delineated content calendar.
3. **Mobilization:** Mobilizing your flock of internal and external advocates, managing their participation with precision, then watching it multiply and take on a life of its own!

Yes, LinkedIn Sales Solutions had more resources than most companies to throw at a lightning strike and heartbeat campaign. But the point for any company is first to generate as big a jolt of electricity about the category as possible, then to follow it up with a constant rhythm of impressions that drives the concept into your audience's brains and creates a sense of inevitability about the category.

How to Woo Analysts

One last important piece of the *go* phase of a category roll-out: Take your category story to industry analysts.

This is particularly important for tech companies selling to businesses. Firms such as Gartner and Forrester are seen as labelers, validators, and arbiters of market categories. Their analysts regularly issue reports about categories and identify the companies in them and their relative positions—who's leading the category, who's challenging, who's falling behind, and so on. Those analysts also love to identify and name new and emerging categories.

It's an odd relationship. Categories don't need analysts to validate them to exist, but validation helps a category prosper. Business buyers often look to analyst reports to help them decide what to purchase. If a category isn't recognized by analysts, business buyers may not be aware of it, or will think it's not important or is still unproven.

So if you're creating a new category, you want to get analysts to validate it, but you can't really ask them to validate it because they want to be the ones discovering and naming a new category. You may have to play a little game to get an analyst to think they've discovered what you're already doing.

In his past years in marketing roles, Mike talked often with analysts. In Kevin's career as a journalist, he often interviewed analysts. And in our category design work, we've helped many companies interact with analysts to get a category recognized. Here are some useful ideas:

Help the analyst get ahead of the curve. It's their job to know about emerging technologies, and they get recognition for being the first to identify an important new category. Tell the analyst that you're developing a new category of product or service, and you want to let them in on it early. Brief them under embargo before you launch. Language like: "We're building a new market category, and I know you're going to want to add us to an existing category, but we want to work with you so you can be known as the analyst who named something new."

You're not there to sell; you're there to inform. Rely on the POV's story. That helps keep you out of sales mode. You're helping the analyst see that the category will be important. If you're the one who articulates the category, the analyst will likely see your company as its leader.

Bring proof. You're pitching something new, so you may not have rocketing sales or engagement figures. But statistics and graphs might help solidify the case for the problem. Make sure that the proof is third-party, reliable, and sourced. Don't throw out vague numbers you can't back up.

Pull together whatever you can to show impending demand for the category. That could include customers or partners asking for the category, media mentions, or me-too competitors. Refer to adjacent categories that the analyst has written about and detail key differences.

Choose your analyst wisely. You only need one analyst to catch on and validate your category. Better to pick a target than try them all. Research who has published reports about categories that may be close to yours. Or find a younger, entrepreneurial analyst who may be looking to make a splash by identifying an emerging category no one else has thought about yet. When you decide on the right analyst to approach, read that analyst's reports and present to them in their language. And ask questions like: "What are you seeing in adjacent spaces?" and "Where would you slot this if it was a trend?" Most analysts want to bring you value, too.

Don't sweat the category name. Again, a lot of analysts want to believe that the category is their idea. And they often want to be the ones to name it. Yes, you might have spent a lot of time and energy debating your category name and pushing it in decks and messages and ads. But allow the category name to be fungible as long as it communicates what the category is about. If an analyst wants to give it a slightly different label, consider going with it. For that matter, once the category is let loose in the market, customers or others may start calling it something different from what you imagined. That's OK, too. The goal is to make the category come alive and then to win it over time. Keep the company steered toward that goal, and don't fight small battles that won't matter.

It's also worth noting that a meeting with an industry analyst is not just a one-way road. The feedback you get about your category, product, and POV can be extremely valuable. "Gartner's greatest strength is in having information from both sides of the market," Gartner analyst Dan Gottleib told Mike on a *Category Thinkers* podcast. The analysts are always talking to vendors like you, and to buyers looking for solutions to their problems. "The process of going through that is actually a great indirect feedback tool," Gottleib said. "Do they get it? Are they asking questions? I had a vendor recently do a briefing, and they got extremely frustrated because the analysts didn't get it, and they saw it revealed a little bit more about these executives than it did about the analyst. Because the executives realized that they had been talking in a bubble, and they didn't have the perspective yet to know where they really fit. I think that's an underrated use of the briefing system."[6]

Use analysts to help you. And then if you get one of the big analyst firms to bless your category and stick your company at the top of it . . . that's a big step toward winning the dominant design over time.

9

The Dominant Design Is Everything

In the fall of 1985, when Kevin was a rookie journalist at *USA Today*, an editor assigned him to write a feature story about the Zamboni company.

He didn't understand then—but of course does now—that the Zamboni is one of the all-time great stories of a startup creating a new market category, winning the dominant design, and milking that win for more than seventy-five years.

If you are reading this and have never been to an ice rink, a Zamboni is the machine that drives around on the ice, scraping off the top layer and adding a new layer of water, making a clean sheet of ice in ten or fifteen minutes.

Strangely enough, the Frank J. Zamboni & Company was

founded not in Canada but in Los Angeles, and is still based there. The LA connection is an important part of the story.

Kevin flew to LA and met with the Zamboni machine inventor, Frank Zamboni, who was eighty-four at the time. (He died in 1988.) His son, Richard, was running day-to-day operations, and as of this writing is still chairman and president. The Zamboni building wasn't flashy—more like a giant auto repair shop combined with an ice rink. There had to be a rink for testing the machines, though sometimes the three-ton machines were taken for test drives on the street outside, which was a hell of a sight.

In the practice of category design, and according to the category creation formula, companies should start by focusing on the problem to be solved, and understand how the context around that problem is either creating new problems or new ways to solve the old problem.

If you understand the problem and context, you'll see the innovation and business that can be built to solve the problem. And if you do that, you'll see how to create a new category of product or service.

Back in the 1930s, before electric refrigerators had become common in homes, the Zamboni family operated a business in LA making ice blocks that went into home iceboxes—the refrigerators of the day. But by 1939, electric refrigerators were catching on and the Zamboni ice-making business was melting away. So the company pivoted: It used its freezing equipment to build a year-round recreational ice rink in the city.

That's when Frank Zamboni saw the problem he needed

to address. Before the Zamboni, a team of five or six guys would require some ninety minutes to clean the ice with scrapers, shovels, and hoses. The long, labor-intensive resurfacing ordeal meant the rink either would be nonoperational for many hours a day or people would have to skate or play hockey on snow-covered, chopped-up ice. Either choice was terrible for business. "I figured there had to be a way to do the job all at once," Frank Zamboni said.[1]

As the 1940s dawned, Zamboni saw there was new technology he could harness. For instance, four-wheel-drive Jeeps were built for the US Army during World War II. The Jeep's lightweight, four-wheel-drive technology could allow a vehicle to get around an ice surface without sliding on or cracking the ice.

Zamboni started tinkering. In 1949, he finished what he called the Zamboni Model A Ice Resurfacer. It had a Jeep-like chassis. On top was a huge wooden box. The driver sat in the back over a wide planer that scraped the ice. Conveyor belts picked up the shavings and dumped them in the box. At the same time, water tanks bolted to the sides washed the ice, leaving a gleaming smooth surface in a fraction of the time and at a much lower cost than manual methods.

Still, Frank Zamboni was just doing this for the family rink, solving his own problem. He thought he was going to just build one machine, not a category of product. "I had no idea it would be a business itself," he said.

But then things started happening. Famed figure skater Sonja Henie was practicing at the Zambonis' rink and saw the machine and asked Frank to make one for her world tour. Thanks to Henie, the Ice Capades started buying them, too. Then the National Hockey League caught on. By the 1960s, two thousand Zambonis were in operation around the world. The machines made ice sports and rink ownership viable. Hockey, figure skating, speed skating, and other ice activities would all barely exist if not for the Zamboni.

Frank Zamboni had indeed created a new category of product. More importantly, the company saw the opportunity to establish the dominant design and worked doggedly to do that. Zamboni knew that if his company didn't improve its machines and set the standard, others would see an opening to build a different design and steal the leadership position in the new category.

That first Model A looked nothing like the Zamboni machines you see today. It was more like a contraption out of the 1968 movie *Chitty Chitty Bang Bang*. Within five years, though, Zamboni had designed and built three new models. The Model D, introduced in 1953, finally looked more like what you'd see buzzing around a rink now. By 1960, Zamboni had firmly established the dominant design.[2]

When you win the dominant design, you become the rule setter for the category, and the rule setter always has an advantage over everyone else. So while competitors came along and started making ice resurfacers, those machines all looked and operated like Zamboni's machines. They were expected to look and work like Zamboni's machines, and still do.

In fact, you know you've thoroughly won the dominant design when people call even your competitors' products by your name. Zamboni is as much a noun as a brand. (As Mike likes to point out, these are called proprietary eponyms. Others include google, kleenex, xerox, and, believe it or not, heroin—once a Bayer pharmaceutical product.)

Now, after seventy-five years, the Zamboni company is still dominating the space. Zamboni continues to use its dominant design position to set the rules for the category. In 2019, it started offering electric Zambonis. Any competitor has had to do the same.

For what it's worth, in case you want to see that first Zamboni Model A, it was bought by the Los Angeles Kings hockey team, which put it on display in a museum at LA Kings Iceland.

The Ultimate Goal

If a company or organization does everything in this book, it will likely develop a clear insight into the category it can create. But that's just the beginning. The ultimate goal is to win the dominant design. And that takes relentless execution on the category strategy, often for years.

That means constantly innovating and evolving and setting the category rules. It means pulling competitors into the category—because a category of one is not a category that matters—yet then continuing to make those competitors subservient to your dominant design.

As we noted about Paul Geroski's research, there is no single playbook for this. Every company executes in its own way, with variations depending on size, industry, product, culture, location, and more. But make no mistake: The enduring, most admired, and most valuable companies are the ones that execute on a category creation strategy and win the dominant design over time. They are the companies whose brands everyone knows—names like Apple, Salesforce, Amazon, Uber, IKEA, Costco, and Coca-Cola.

Why do some companies come up with a great POV, rally around a category strategy, do all the right things in the first year, but then eventually fail to win the dominant design?

Usually, they give in to what we called *gravity* in *Play Bigger*. Gravity is the day-to-day, relentless and very real pull of running a company. Gravity can take hold when a company feels the need to chase short-term revenue or add a feature that a customer wants, even if the feature doesn't fit with the category strategy. Gravity comes in the form of decisions about hiring, finances, legal matters, the food in the break area, the color of the walls. Gravity can compel a leadership team to give up too soon if they don't see the category taking off.

So not only is it necessary to stay faithful to the category strategy and POV, it's important to recognize the forces of gravity and manage them so they don't prevent you from winning the dominant design.

As we described in chapter 6, concerning economist Geroski's work, your category strategy is not a success until you've won the dominant design and can see the value of the category soar while the number of competitors collapses.

That's when your company ends up in position to take

most of the category's economics. And that's the point of this whole exercise.

Apple's Relentless Pursuit of the Dominant Design

We used Apple and its iPhone as a way to illustrate the theories of Paul Geroski and the power of winning the dominant design. While Jobs's introduction of the iPhone in 2007 was dramatic and historic, the whole world didn't instantly fall in line with the iPhone's design and reject all the other designs that came before. In fact, if Apple had stopped with what it unveiled on day one, it's unlikely the iPhone would've won the dominant design.

Apple systematically and relentlessly built on the first iPhone and executed a series of lightning strikes and heartbeats for almost a decade, establishing a sense in the industry and among consumers that it knew how the category of smartphone should work. Apple ultimately convinced the public that the iPhone was the dominant design.

Along the way, Apple kept the iPhone on the front edge of the adjacent possible, constantly pushing the technology just past what people were already experiencing and advancing our comfort level with what a smartphone could do. Today, if a smartphone and its ecosystem doesn't look and work much like an iPhone, it has zero chance of making a dent in the smartphone category.

Here's a quick look at the procession of important Apple

advances—a series of lightning strikes—that ultimately won the dominant design for the smartphone category:

2007: The original iPhone was unveiled by Steve Jobs in a massively successful strike that captivated the industry and consumers. The first iPhone broke new ground (pushed the adjacent possible!) with its full-glass screen with a keyboard on the screen. (A lot of people, used to tactile keyboards, didn't like that.) The phone had a camera on the back, could connect to the internet, and could hold several hundred songs. It worked on Apple's new iPhone OS—later just called iOS. Overall, this first iPhone introduced the idea that a smartphone should be an all-in-one device that's super easy to use.

2008: Apple introduced the App Store—a new concept that opened up the phone to third-party developers. The company ran ads (category design heartbeats) that famously declared, "There's an app for that!" The App Store effectively de-positioned most of the smartphones on the market because those competitors didn't have an ecosystem. You couldn't add third-party apps to most phones. As the public started to embrace apps, any phone that didn't offer them fell out of the race for the dominant design.

Also in 2008, Google introduced the Android operating system and Play Store. Notably, the Android OS and ecosystem was a copy of Apple's design. Far from threatening the iPhone, Android's bow to Apple actually helped solidify Apple's position as the dominant design and the category rule setter.

2010: Apple added a front-facing camera and introduced

FaceTime. Apple then had a proprietary way for people to talk to each other with video, setting another expectation for the category and again eliminating more competitors. Face-Time also created a reason for friends and family to all get iPhones, since FaceTime wouldn't work with any other kind of phone.

2011: Apple introduced Siri, the first mainstream voice assistant. Even though Siri was more of a novelty than truly useful, it again set new rules for the category (people expected phones to have a voice assistant) and stretched the adjacent possible (which made Siri seem exciting and cool yet comprehensible).

While these big announcements every year were all attention-grabbing lightning strikes, Apple had not yet solidified the dominant design, three years after the iPhone's introduction. Nokia's Symbian operating system was on about 60 percent of phones worldwide in 2010. BlackBerry still sold phones with external keyboards. Microsoft was pushing its Windows Phone. But by now the Apple ecosystem and design had the momentum, amplified by Android's copycat success.

2013: The iPhone 5S came out with Touch ID, allowing users to open their phones with a fingerprint. Compared to previous advances, this one was more incremental, but it advanced the rules for smartphones and kept Apple in the lead for dominant design.

2014: Apple Pay was introduced, creating the idea that a phone should also be your wallet—again advancing the dominant design and pushing the adjacent possible. The public quickly came to expect to be able to pay with a phone. Google would introduce Android Pay a year later. An important sign, as noted earlier, that consumers had become comfortable with a dominant design: In 2014 the smartphone market was more than ten times larger than on the day Jobs introduced the iPhone.

2015–16: Big iPhone innovations became rarer and more spaced out. Apple started offering phones with larger screens—a rare instance when Apple was a follower in the category. Others had been making them for a while and as people watched more video on phones, they asked for bigger screens.

Yet this time period is when it could be said that Apple decisively won the dominant design. By 2016, Nokia would discontinue Symbian, BlackBerry would stop making its classic versions with external keyboards, while Microsoft would kill Windows Phone in 2017. Apple's iPhone and Google's Android took over the market, crowding out almost every other kind of smartphone.

In 2017, Android was on more phones worldwide than Apple's iOS, because Android was on every model of phone that wasn't Apple. But Apple retained pricing power and, as noted earlier, by some estimates took more than 90 percent of the smartphone sector profits. Apple has continued to this day to set the public's expectations for what a smartphone should be.

In other words, Apple utterly won the dominant design around 2016, nine years after the first iPhone debuted. Over those nine years, the company relentlessly developed the iPhone's design and features and told us about them with a rhythm of lightning strikes and heartbeat campaigns. It continuously set the rules for the category and made all others follow them.

What does the iPhone story mean for your company? Identifying and defining a category and launching a category-creating product really is the beginning. Expect that it will take years of focus, rule-setting, and innovation to decisively win the dominant design. Through that time, never take your eye off the ball. Your ultimate goal is to develop a category that matters and become the company that controls the dominant design.

That's total victory. That's when the company becomes valuable, admired, enduring, and important.

After all, wasn't that your goal when you picked up this book?

10

DIY Category Design

So you and your team have decided to apply strategic category design. You could bring in someone to facilitate the process, and there's a lot of value in getting an outside perspective. But you've decided to do it in-house. To help guide you, let's take the details from the previous chapters and lay out how to go about that, step by step.

Why Do It

A fundamental rule of strategic category design is that the CEO must drive it. No matter who first suggests it, category design won't work unless the CEO buys in and then wins buy-in from the core leadership team. Strategic category design is ultimately a whole-company endeavor.

The CEO and leadership team are more likely to buy in if they clearly understand what problem the company has that category design can help remedy. (That's always been the first step in category design: knowing the problem to solve.) In chapter 2, we discussed eight syndromes that can get in the way of successfully creating and winning a market category. Discuss them and see which ones seem to fit your situation. Sometimes it's a combination of more than one. Or perhaps you see a different problem that we haven't identified. No matter what, understanding and articulating why it's worth going through the process will help motivate the team.

Here, again and briefly, are the syndromes:

Vision entropy: The company has a big long-term vision but there is concern that the team and partners are not completely aligned and pulling in the same direction for the long haul.

Build it and they will come: Some companies build an amazing product but have a hard time telling potential customers in plain language why people need such a product.

Spinning strategic compass: As companies scale, hire new leaders, make acquisitions, and start new product lines, the mission and goals can grow branches that become misaligned.

Category jail: Analysts, investors, the press, or potential customers keep shoving you into an existing category that you don't want to be in.

Chronic fatigue syndrome: Sometimes companies that have been successful for a long time need a next act. There's nothing terribly wrong, but the sense of mission and forward drive seem to be stuck in a low gear.

Impractical futurism: Some founders so clearly see the future, they believe it's already here—and then they build a futuristic product that doesn't quite work well enough or that potential customers don't yet understand.

No time to lose: A company may need a competitive boost to increase its odds of winning the category while de-positioning contenders. This is often the case in a hot new category that does not yet have a dominant design winner.

Fundraising-story anemia: The company knows what category it wants to build yet has difficulty putting together a powerful investor deck or S1 that tells that story.

When to Do Strategic Category Design

Well, if you're asking us, we'd say that every new company should go through a strategic category design exercise right from the start, and then appoint a chief category officer who will think about and drive the category mission every day. Most companies will benefit from doing this sooner rather than later.

But, assuming that's not where you are, there is otherwise no one absolutely right or wrong time to work on category design.

Category design is particularly valuable to early-stage

companies trying to define themselves and to companies that are about to raise funding or go public. We have also seen category design give new life to decades-old companies and help major corporations give definition to a new innovation.

There is no wrong time for a company that desires to define, develop, and win a new market category. There is only a wrong kind of company. If a company's strategy is to win a small share of a big established market by competing on price or features, then that company is not out to create or win a market category, so there's no need for category design.

Who Should Be Involved

If a company is determined to stay true to the category design process, the CEO must take the lead and choose the team to go through the process.

Ideally, the team will be a minimum of four people and a maximum of twelve. Fewer than four, there's not enough discussion and energy in the room. More than a dozen gets unwieldy—everyone wants to give their input, and then every matter takes forever to discuss.

The team should represent different aspects of the company. It's good to have the chief executive officer, chief marketing officer, head of product, head of sales, and any cofounders in the room. Others to consider (if the company has these roles) are the chief operating officer, chief people officer, chief financial officer, legal counsel, and head of business development or chief evangelist. Some companies may want to include a lead investor or an important member of the board.

The key criteria for the CEO when choosing should be: Whom would I want in the room to make a critical decision about the company's future?

Significantly, the team should be able to assemble in person and commit to two full-day workshops. Yes, it's possible to run the category design process virtually, over Zoom or Teams or whatever. But it won't work as well as having everyone together live. The category design process is not just about coming up with a POV and category strategy. An important element is the team alignment around a shared mission—to build consensus on every decision. That's more likely to be achieved if the team is interacting in person.

We discussed in chapters 1 and 7 how we take companies through an intensive four-day strategic category design workshop. Here, we pull together those elements with a few other tips on doing it yourself.

Workshop 1: Category Discovery

You've chosen the team. You've picked a time and place. Line up a conference room or some other setting where the team can work together comfortably, uninterrupted, for long hours. Have a way to project slides; you'll need that at least for the POV presentation. Make sure there's a whiteboard—sometimes it can help to diagram or write out an idea.

Appoint a lead facilitator, someone respected who can guide the discussion. That could be the CEO, but it doesn't have to be. Also appoint a lead person who will later draft the POV. The best choice is someone who is both a good conceptual thinker and a good writer. It should not be the chief facilitator. The POV writer will need to listen hard and take notes while participating in the discussion.

An important instruction: The goal of the meeting is to identify and define a significant market category that the company can create and/or win. You're not there to come up with a marketing campaign to sell your specific product or brand. In fact, it can be helpful to pretend your company doesn't exist. Instead, the team should feel that they are there to discover a category opportunity and then to envision the company that can seize that opportunity.

Ready to start the meeting? Then begin with a discussion of the category formula:

$$f(\text{category}) = \text{context} + \text{missing} + \text{innovation}$$

First, do a deep dive on *context*. Resist moving on from that topic until you feel like you all really understand how the context is changing around your target customers.

That should lead you to insights about what is *missing*. What problem do your customers have that's never been adequately solved, but now can be solved because of changes in technology or society? Or is there a big new problem to be solved that's been created by the changes in context? Have the changes in context created a problem that your audience doesn't yet even realize it has?

Once you can describe what's missing, the basic outlines of the *innovation* you can build to solve for the missing should seem obvious. Dig in further and discuss what that innovation should look like—no matter who builds it. Again, this is not about your company. It's about truth. If you now see something that must exist, you'll know you must build it.

Next, consider the adjacent possible. Discuss how to make sure the innovation lands there. If it does, it will be different from anything else on the market. But it won't be so different that you can't make it work, or people won't get it.

Once you see how it can land in the adjacent possible, discuss the vision for the future. How do you build on your product over the next five years? What's the journey you want to take your customers on?

Finally, consider the Geroski graph. It's helpful to know if you are creating an entirely new category. Or maybe you realize you are entering an emerging yet still chaotic category that is waiting for a dominant design to emerge. If so, discuss whether your company can step in and win that dominant design. On the other hand, if you conclude that the category already has a dominant design, know that you will have a hard time unseating the winner, and that your strategy instead might be to nail down the number two position—a Lyft to Uber; an Android to Apple.

Only then discuss why your company is best positioned to create or win this category. What special capabilities or position do you have? What would you need to upgrade in order to win this category?

All you discuss will be fuel for the POV. One good way to end the day is for someone in the room to talk through what they think the POV will say, and see if everyone agrees.

POV Writing

The day after the first session, the lead writer should start drafting the POV. A strong writer may prefer to work on it alone. A more collaborative writer may want to lock themselves in a room with one or two others. Either way, it's good to start on day two, when the ideas are fresh and electric.

You also want to keep the momentum going. Speed and momentum keep the process on track and focused. When we work with companies, we write the POV in two days and schedule the workshop to review the POV for the following day. That pace may not work for every company, but we strongly advise leaving no more than a week to draft the POV, and hold the review meeting immediately after the POV is ready.

While writing the POV, remember the superhero movie plot structure.

Again, the POV must describe the truth about a solution that needs to exist. The POV is not your company's marketing message.

To properly do its work, a POV should be at least five hundred words. To keep people from feeling it's too long, keep it to a thousand words or less.

The draft will not be perfect. It never is. That's OK. It's

meant to capture what the team discussed on day one. It should be provocative, so it prompts more discussion in the next meeting.

Once the draft is ready, put it into a series of slides, with only one or two sentences on each slide on a blank background. The deck is not meant to be pretty. You want the team to pay attention only to the words.

Now you're ready for the second meeting of the team.

Workshop 2: The POV Session

It's essential that all of the same team members who assembled for the first category design session also attend this session. The process of going through this together, and jointly developing and signing off on the POV, generates a bond among the team and alignment around the mission. That alignment will pay off when the CEO asks the team members to evangelize the POV throughout the company. It will pay off when the company implements the category strategy and has to execute, in a coordinated way, for years ahead in order to win the dominant design.

So assemble the team—in the same room as before, if possible. Fire up the POV slide deck, showing it on a screen so everyone can see it. We gave you brief instructions in chapter 7 on how to run this part of the meeting, but here is more detail:

The POV writer, or one of the POV collaborators, then should toggle through the POV slide by slide while reading each slide aloud. Everyone else should sit back and take it in. Closed laptops. Stashed phones. No note taking. Just have everyone listen.

When the initial reading of the POV is finished, the lead facilitator should pause, then ask for broad feedback. Don't try to address details yet. Talk about whether the story makes sense. Does it reflect who you are as a company and the opportunity you see? Does it capture the first day's conversation? What do you like most? What feels wrong? How does the proposed category name feel? (If the category name doesn't feel right, set that discussion aside for now. You can write a POV and leave the category name blank. Come back to it later, once the POV is nearly done, and the right category name often pops out.)

Let that conversation play out until it gets repetitive or seems to run out of steam. Then show and read the POV slides again. This time, suggest that everyone make note of specific things they want to address. Read the whole thing before asking for any feedback. Talk about it broadly again. Keep in mind this is only the second time that most in the room are absorbing the POV. The POV writer should take notes about what is being said.

Then it's time to address specifics. Go back again to the first slide. Read each slide out loud and ask for discussion. Don't try to edit or write as a group—that leads to the too-many-chefs problem. Instead, put notes about the feedback in comments on the slides. The POV writer may also take their own notes.

This can feel tedious and maybe even painful. But do this

through the whole POV. The lead writer now has feedback to work with.

The next step is to use the feedback to revise the POV. Consider pausing the meeting while the writer or collaborators find a quiet spot to make the revisions. Bring everyone back once the revisions are done, and read through the whole POV again, slide by slide. Open up the discussion; this time through, most of the changes should be minor, and the group can make them together.

However you do it, the goal for this day's meeting is to work through the POV as a team until every person in the room feels good about the outcome. Imagine the men who gathered to draft the US Declaration of Independence in 1776, finally agreeing on the text and all enthusiastically signing their name to it. That's the feeling you're going for in the room. In fact, as a way to close out the meeting and get everyone's buy-in, you could print out the POV on nice paper and have each team member sign it.

Now you have a POV that clearly tells anyone why this category of product or service must exist, the problem it solves, the rules for solving it, and why your company is best positioned to develop the category. Lock it down. Resist the urge to tweak it. It's important that the whole team feels they created every word of the POV. Don't put that alignment at risk. Embrace the POV and get ready to evangelize it.

Before the team disperses, the CEO has one last task: to name one person who will be in charge of the rollout of the POV and category strategy. Every member of the team will have a role to play, but it's good to have someone coordinating.

Ready, Set, Go

Once the POV is locked down, the first task goes to the company's lawyers: Protect any terms in the POV that you don't want others to claim. As noted in chapter 7, protect the category name with an intent-to-use filing so no one else can trademark it. Buy URLs of the category name. Similarly protect other valuable terms in the POV, like the name of a thing or the name of the villain. The whole point is to keep these terms in public use, because it's good for the category if anyone can use those terms.

Then it's time to get the rest of the company on board, as described in chapter 8. Infuse the POV into the culture. Have every part of the company develop plans for making the POV a reality.

Set a date for that first lightning strike, when you will tell the world about the category and your role in it. The product team needs to make sure the product lives up to the POV promise in time for the strike. Marketing must create messaging and a new website derived from the POV. Sales should redo their sales decks; the executive team should redo the investor pitch.

Plan and execute a lightning strike when all of the elements come together to make an initial big splash. Then keep the momentum going with a heartbeat campaign culminating in regular, significant strikes.

The Long Game

Never forget that the company's mission is to develop the category, remain its leader, set its rules, and eventually win the dominant design. That will take years of execution on the category strategy.

Reinforce the category strategy as the company's North Star, even as gravity pulls company leaders into managing the day-to-day.

Continue to build on the original category-defining product so it stays aligned with the adjacent possible and ahead of competitors. Make sure you set the rules and pace of the category's development. Continue to tell the story of where you will take the category in the years ahead. Take your target customers on a journey from what they did before the category existed, to how they will do things—and how their work or lives will be better—as the category blooms.

Regularly schedule leadership meetings to reevaluate the category and the company's role in it. Revisit the category formula. One truism in life is that context constantly changes, so if the context changes, then it will impact the missing and the innovation. Staying on top of those shifts will help keep your company in the category lead.

Stay true to your strategy until the market settles on your dominant design while competing designs fall away and the category's economics skyrocket.

Strategic Category Design for the Individual: The OK Go Story

This book is aimed primarily at businesses. But it's an easy leap to graft the same concepts onto an individual's career.

One path to success is to become very good at an existing category of job—an exceptional heart surgeon, an exceptional car mechanic, an exceptional baseball player. But often a path to outsize success is to create a category of your own that matters, even if it only matters within a niche. If you solve a significant problem that no one else can solve, you by definition become valuable.

The category creation formula can help anyone see a productive path forward.

Start with context.

If you work at a big company, develop an understanding of how the context around the people you work for and with is changing. If you're thinking of starting a business in your town or region, dig into how the context in your community is changing. Is the new context opening up new ways to solve an old problem? Is it creating new problems that no one is solving?

Great changes in context open up new categories of work waiting to be created. As we write this, technologies such as artificial intelligence, along with global shifts in politics and trade, are stirring up some of the greatest changes in context in history.

Understand the changes in context around you, and you will see what's missing. If you see what's missing, you will see how to be innovative about what you do in order to address the missing. And if you can do that, you will create a valuable category for yourself.

You won't be one of many accountants or journalists or line managers or welders—you'll become one of the only ones who do what you do. You'll create a new category and position yourself as its leader.

As a different and fun way to close this out, you can see how individual category creation played out in the success of musician and songwriter Damian Kulash and his band, OK Go.[1]

Rewind back to 2005. The band's second album, *Oh No*, had just been released. Its first album hadn't gotten much attention. The context around the music industry was changing dramatically. Digital downloads were a new thing—first came the pirate versions like Napster, which caught the record industry off guard, followed by industry-sanctioned versions led by Apple with its iTunes store. Digital downloads made it easy for fans to cherry-pick individual songs to buy, hurting CD sales—and at the time, record companies were making most of their profits off CDs. MTV had been around for almost twenty-five years, playing highly produced music videos from popular bands, but in 2005 YouTube had just been founded, opening a way for even little-known bands to post videos that they could make, well, in someone's backyard.

Such changes in context open up opportunities to create new categories.

Now, Kulash, as you might imagine, didn't call a meeting with his other band members (Tim Nordwind, Dan Konopka, and Andy Ross) and go through a category design exercise. But they stumbled into a category creation opportunity and then, a bit like Apple with its iPhone, relentlessly built on it for years.

After making their second album, the band planned on a tour to support it. They wanted to do something onstage that would leave an impression, and recalled that they'd done a near-impromptu silly dance on stage a few years earlier that got the audience cheering. Maybe, Kulash thought, they should end their upcoming shows with something similar. Kulash called his sister, dancer Trish Sie, to help. She flew to Kulash's house in Chicago with her toddler. In the yard, the guys ran through what she choreographed. Once they had their routine down, the guys set up a video camera on a tripod and taped it—"just to see what it looked like," as Kulash recalled.

And it looked like fun. The lone video camera rolled. The dance was done in one take, no editing. It looked totally homegrown. OK Go's label, EMI, had nothing to do with the video, but once some of its executives saw it, they encouraged interns to post it on the internet. Kulash burned the video on CDs and handed them out at concerts. "We'd give them to the kids who looked the nerdiest," Kulash said.

In the changing context of the time, it all landed perfectly. The stunt was honest, funny, dumb, much like what was getting posted on early YouTube. The video did something new at the time: It went viral. It got millions of views, and OK Go found themselves invited to be on *Good Morning America*. Concerts started selling out.

If Kulash was not a category thinker, he might have considered the viral dance a fluke and gone on just trying to be a rock star hoping for a hit song. Instead, he followed where the fluke was taking him.

The band again called in Kulash's sister. "We brainstormed on how to ratchet it up a notch. It had to be some sort of systems thing," Kulash said. "She came up with the treadmill idea."

You may remember OK Go's treadmill dance to their song "Here It Goes Again." One camera; one take. The band had to do a crazy, injury-waiting-to-happen dance perfectly, hopping on and off the kind of treadmills you see in a gym—while the treadmill floors were moving. The video exploded on YouTube. Kulash got booked on *The Colbert Report* and *The Tonight Show*. Sales of the band's music took off. "It fits YouTube like a glove," author Henry Jenkins said at the time. "It has an authenticity that comes from being slightly crudely made. It feels like it's from the bottom up, which is hard to pull off."[2]

In October 2006, Google bought YouTube for $1.7 billion. Kulash half joked, "YouTube got sold for a few billion dollars, and we are their poster children. The dots connected."

In fact, OK Go's video stunts landed smack dab in the adjacent possible. If OK Go had made those videos a few years earlier, the videos might've just been something that got passed around among friends and family. A few years later, and the videos might've gotten lost amid the many other videos on YouTube. But by accident, OK Go landed on the adjacent possible. It made all the difference.

To Kulash's credit, he and the rest of the band understood they were handed an opportunity to be a new category of music artist—a category you might call video-stunt rock band. It's a category OK Go created and still dominates, though it's a niche category that doesn't seem to be overly populated.

In the years since, Kulash, Sie, and the others have done a zero-gravity video, using one of those planes that gives you about thirty seconds of weightlessness at a time. They built an insanely complex Rube Goldberg contraption that rolled to their tune "This Too Shall Pass." They created an elaborately choreographed Busby Berkeley–like spectacle while riding tiny scooters. Most people know the videos better than the songs the videos feature. And, two decades after the backyard video, Kulash hasn't stopped executing on his category. He and the band continue to pump out TikTok videos, and in 2025 launched a tour—actually called "And the Adjacent Possible Tour."

OK Go has never released a true hit song. If Kulash had relied on being one of countless numbers of participants in the well-established category of rock star (or even a subcategory like power-pop rock star), OK Go probably would today have a small fan base and likely never would have appeared on national television.

But Kulash took his own route. In the context of changing times, he staked out a category for OK Go that was all their own. He followed through by continuing to innovate and set the rules. It's not a huge category. He's not a billionaire. Still, creating, developing, and winning a new category—one that landed on the adjacent possible at just the right time—made all the difference.

It can make all the difference for anyone.

Acknowledgments

Kevin and Mike thank the company leaders we've worked with over the years. Every one of them has deepened our understanding of both the theories behind and practicalities of strategic category design. Those lessons are what make up this book. We look forward to learning even more as we work with leaders we've not yet met.

Thank you, also, to the category design community, especially Christopher Lochhead and Al Ramadan. Ever since *Play Bigger*, they've helped make category design an integral part of the conversation in the tech ecosystem and have always been supportive of us and our work. And we are grateful to the many, many others who call themselves category designers and contribute to growing the . . . well . . . category of category design.

Thank you, Hollis Heimbouch and Jim Levine. Hollis edited *Play Bigger* and edited this book. Her support and guidance have been life-changing for Kevin—and now for Mike, too. Jim has been Kevin's agent for more than fifteen years, and represented the two of us for this book. If there were a book agent hall of fame, he'd be inducted—if he ever retires.

This book, like most meaningful things in life, is the product of many generous hands, open minds, and big hearts—not all mentioned here.

From Kevin

An enormous thank-you to my partner, Katherine Oliver, for her enthusiastic support, love, friendship, and shared taste for really good tequila. Thank you to my brothers, Scott and Dave, because, when I think about it, they had more to do with the way I think and what I laugh at than anyone. Of course, thank you to the rest of my family for always rallying around me and each other, across the generations.

And special thanks to Hemant Taneja, my authoring partner through four books over the past decade. I learned so much from working with Hemant and the people around him at General Catalyst and GC's portfolio companies, and that has profoundly shaped my thinking about building enduring, important companies.

From Mike

First and always, to my wife and best friend, Linda—thank you for being my constant source of love, laughter, and perspective. Nothing I've done—or ever will do—happens without her support and belief in me. To my parents, Roger and Mary, whose quiet strength and unwavering values shaped who I am. And especially for my father, who taught me the importance of leadership—not through lectures, but through example.

To the late, great Dick Morley—my friend and mentor, my first investor, and the original believer in me. He saw something in me before I fully saw it in myself. Thank you for nudging me onto the entrepreneurial path. I owe more than I can say for that first spark (and check).

To the original *Play Bigger* crew: Thank you for the belief in me that I could help shape the future of category design, and for suggesting that I partner with Kevin to form Category Design Advisors. What a ride.

For all who impacted me over the years, I'm grateful beyond words.

Notes

1 | The Power of Strategic Category Design

1. A nod to Stephen Covey's *The 7 Habits of Highly Effective People.* Habit number two, according to the book and the FranklinCovey website: "Begin With the End in Mind is about having a plan. If we don't make a conscious effort to visualize who we are and what we want in life, then we empower other people and circumstances to shape us instead. This habit is about identifying where we want to go and who we want to be." And that is at the very core of strategic category design. See: https://www.franklincovey.com/courses/the-7-habits/habit-2.

2. This section is from CDA's interactions with Prescryptive over time, and an interview with Chris Blackley by Kevin Maney, 2024.

3. Google is now being challenged by a new category of product that's less about search than answers. That category was initially created by ChatGPT and now has a number of companies competing to win the category. No telling yet how it will turn out, but, as we noted in *Play Bigger,* category winners don't usually get displaced by a challenger within the category—they get displaced by a new category. Al Ramadan, Dave Peterson, Christopher Lochhead, and Kevin Maney, *Play Bigger: How Pirates, Dreamers, and Innovators Create and Dominate Markets* (Harper Business, 2016).

4. A totally defensible figure seems nearly impossible to come by, and changes all the time. But in 2016, BMO Capital Markets published the 103.6 percent figure: https://9to5mac.com/2016/11/04 /apple-iphone-captures-103-6-of-smartphone-industry-profits-in -q3-according-to-analyst-estimates/. In 2023, Counterpoint Research said that Apple and Samsung together took in 96 percent of the industry's operating profits: https://wccftech.com/apple-and -samsung-net-a-crazy-96-of-operating-profits-while-rest-of-the -manufacturers-are-fighting-for-leftovers/. In 2024, Needham said that the iPhone in 2025 would account for 89 percent to 96 percent of Apple's total profits: https://www.pws.io/apple-iphone-to-fuel-96 -of-2025-revenue-analyst-says-a-safer-bet-than-ai-heavy-amazon -alphabet-micro. Other analysts through the years have estimated Apple wins north of two-thirds of the industry's profits.

5. Mary Meisenzahl, "Hard-Seltzer Sales Are Surging. Here Are the 3 Most Popular Brands and 2 Newcomers Hoping to Chip Away at Their Dominance," *Business Insider,* June 28, 2021, https://www .businessinsider.com/white-claw-truly-bud-light-most-popular -hard-seltzers-and-newer-brands-2021-6.

2 | Conditions for Strategic Category Design

1. Scott Kupor, *Secrets of Sand Hill Road: Venture Capital and How to Get It* (Portfolio, 2019), beginning at location 677, Kindle.

2. This section derives from Kevin Maney's article, "Strategic Category Design and Vision Entropy: Insights from Teledesic's Demise," which in turn was derived from Maney's ongoing coverage of Teledesic for *USA Today* in the 1990s: https://www.categorydesignadvisors.com /vision-entropy-teledesic/.

3. A tip of the cap here to John Rougeux, who worked with us at CDA for about a year and contributed to the shaping of the syndromes.

4. Cherlynn Low, "The Humane AI Pin is the Solution to None of Technology's Problems," *Engadget,* April 11, 2024, https://www.engadget .com/the-humane-ai-pin-is-the-solution-to-none-of-technologys -problems-120002469.html.

5. Michael Olenick, "Segway Case Study: Avoiding the Fate of the Segway Electric Scooter," *Blue Ocean*, undated, https://www.blueoceanstrategy.com/blog/segway-case-study-avoiding-fate-of-segway-electric-scooter.

6. This section derives from Kevin Maney's "Why There's No Market in MLB for the Knuckleball: A Case Could Be Made for the Slowest Pitch in Baseball," *Front Row Seat for a Revolution*, August 23, 2023, https://kevinmaney.substack.com/p/why-theres-no-market-in-mlb-for-the.

3 | Market/Product Fit

1. Jack Ewing, "Electric Cars Are Suddenly Becoming Affordable," *The New York Times*, June 3, 2024, https://www.nytimes.com/2024/06/03/business/electric-cars-becoming-affordable.html.

2. Craig Jamieson, "Top Gear's Top 9: Electric Cars That Tried and Failed," *BBC TopGear*, undated, https://www.topgear.com/car-news/electric/top-gears-top-9-electric-cars-tried-and-failed.

3. Marc Andreessen, "The Only Thing That Matters," Pmarchive, June 25, 2007, https://pmarchive.com/guide_to_startups_part4.html.

4. "How Category Design and Product-Led Growth Shaped Slack's GTM Strategy w/ Bill Macaitis," *Category Thinkers*, podcast, episode 7, August 1, 2023, https://www.categorythinkers.com/podcast/category-design-bill-macaitis-slack.

5. This section derives from Kevin Maney's "Bigfoot and Me: That Time I Interviewed the Inventor of Monster Trucks and Rode in One During a Show," *Front Row Seat for a Revolution*, January 10, 2024, https://kevinmaney.substack.com/p/bigfoot-and-me.

4 | The Category Creation Formula

1. Transcript of Steve Jobs introducing the iPhone, January 9, 2007, https://singjupost.com/wp-content/uploads/2014/07/Steve-Jobs-iPhone-2007-Presentation-Full-Transcript.pdf.

2. Apple WWDC 2023 Transcript, Rev.com, https://www.rev.com/transcripts/apple-wwdc-2023-transcript.

3. During World War II, Ingvar Kamprad had been involved with two different Swedish fascist groups, though he would later publicly disavow those beliefs. As far as we know, no one boycotts IKEA because its founder got led astray as a teenager.

4. Tom Huddleston Jr., "43-Year-Old Used Her Life Savings to Open a Bar That Only Plays Women's Sports—It Brought in Almost $1 Million in 8 Months," CNBC, April 27, 2023, https://www.cnbc.com/2023/04/27/jenny-nguyen-how-the-sports-bra-became-haven-for-womens-sports-fans.html.

5. Melissa Kravitz Hoeffner, "The Sports Bra, a Women's Sports Bar, Starts Franchising," *Forbes*, September 18, 2024, https://www.forbes.com/sites/melissakravitz/2024/09/18/the-sports-bra-americas-first-womens-sports-bar-starts-franchising/.

6. Gail Moody-Byrd, "Reimagining B2B Selling with Deep Sales and LinkedIn," LinkedIn.com, September 20, 2022, https://www.linkedin.com/business/sales/blog/strategy/introducing-deep-sales-a-new-category.

7. "LinkedIn Sales Solutions Deep Sales Study," Ipsos, February 21, 2024, https://www.ipsos.com/en-us/linkedin-sales-solutions-deep-sales-study.

8. This section draws from Hemant Taneja and Kevin Maney's *Unscaled: How AI and a New Generation of Upstarts Are Creating the Economy of the Future* (PublicAffairs, 2018).

9. Carlota Perez, *Technological Revolutions and Financial Capital: The Dynamics of Bubbles and Golden Ages* (Edward Elgar Publishing, 2003), page 151.

5 | The Adjacent Possible

1. Steven Johnson, *Where Good Ideas Come From: The Natural History of Innovation* (Riverhead Books, 2010), pages 25–28.

2. This section derives from Kevin Maney's "The Little Known and Long

Gone Company That Created the Future of the Olympics," *Front Row Seat for a Revolution*, August 7, 2024, https://kevinmaney.substack .com/p/the-little-known-and-long-gone-company.

3. Tripp Mickle and Erin Griffith, "'This Is Going to Be Painful': How a Bold A.I. Device Flopped," *The New York Times*, June 6, 2024, https://www.nytimes.com/2024/06/06/technology/humane-ai-pin .html.

4. This section derives from Kevin Maney's "The Very No Good Bad Technology That Almost Ruined Hockey," *Front Row Seat for a Revolution*, November 5, 2023, https://kevinmaney.substack.com/p /the-very-no-good-bad-technology-that.

5. Steven Johnson, *Emergence: The Connected Lives of Ants, Brains, Cities, and Software* (Scribner, 2001).

6. You'll have to check daily to see what Tesla is worth. In early 2025, Tesla stock—and thus the company's market value—sank considerably as CEO Elon Musk got involved with the Trump administration.

7. "Configure Price Quote Software Global Strategic Analysis Report 2024: Market to Reach $7.3 Billion by 2030 - Rising Adoption of Automation Solutions in Business Operations," *Yahoo! Finance*, May 22, 2024, https://uk.finance.yahoo.com/news/configure-price -quote-software-global-081400716.html.

6 | The Secret Life of Categories

1. This section derives from Paul Geroski's *The Evolution of New Markets* (Oxford University Press, 2018).

2. This syncs up with the observations of Geoffrey Moore in his classic book *Crossing the Chasm* (Harper Business, 2014), in which he explains that early adopters will take a chance on innovations, but the pragmatic majority prefers incremental improvements to established products and solutions. The trick to avoiding product failure, Moore says, is to overcome the chasm between these two groups. In Geroski's formulation, that happens when a version of that innovation becomes the dominant design.

3. This section derives from Kevin Maney's "When Cell Phones Were Strange," *Front Row Seat for a Revolution*, March 4, 2023, https://kevinmaney.substack.com/p/when-cell-phones-were-strange.

4. Fehim Duzgun and Gonca Telli Yamamoto, "The Effect of Promoter Incentive to the Smartphone Sales in Retail Chains: A Turkish Case," *International Journal of Economics & Management Sciences* 5, no. 6 (2016), https://www.researchgate.net/figure/Number-of-smartphones-sold-to-end-users-worldwide-from-2007-to-2014-in-million-units_fig2_312321048.

5. Kevin Maney, "How White Claw Won and Shaped Its Category," undated, Category Design Advisors blog, https://www.categorydesignadvisors.com/how-white-claw-won-and-shaped-its-category/.

6. Uber's first pitch deck can be found in many places on the internet. One is PitchDeckHunt.com, https://www.pitchdeckhunt.com/pitch-decks/uber.

7. That cycle of new categories arising to beat old ones is well described by Clayton Christensen in *The Innovator's Dilemma: When New Technologies Cause Great Firms to Fail* (Harvard Business Review Press, 2013).

7 | Superhero POVs

1. Sam J. Maglio and Taly Reich, "Feeling Certain: Gut Choice, the True Self, and Attitude Certainty," *Emotion* 19, no. 5 (August 2019): 876–88, https://pubmed.ncbi.nlm.nih.gov/30198736/.

2. Dylan Walsh, "We're More Likely to Stick to Decisions Rooted in Emotions," *Yale Insights*, June 23, 2020, https://insights.som.yale.edu/insights/we-re-more-likely-to-stick-to-decisions-rooted-in-emotions.

3. Robert J. Shiller, *Narrative Economics: How Stories Go Viral and Drive Major Economic Events* (Princeton University Press, 2019), page 86.

4. "The Rider & the Elephant—Jonathan Haidt on Persuasion and Moral Humility," excerpted from *The Tom Woods Show*, podcast, episode 429, June 22, 2015, https://www.youtube.com/watch?v=24adApYh0yc.

5. Daniel Kahneman, *Thinking, Fast and Slow* (Farrar, Straus and Giroux, 2013).

6. Dylan Walsh, "What Separates the Ideas that Endure from Those That Fade?," *Yale Insights*, March 1, 2021, https://insights.som.yale.edu/insights/what-separates-the-ideas-that-endure-from-those-that-fade.

7. Ken Rutsky, "How Category Memetics Can Help a New Category Stick w/ Ken Rutsky," *Category Thinkers*, podcast, episode 29, January 2, 2024, https://www.categorythinkers.com/podcast/how-category-memetics-can-help-a-new-category-stick.

8. Interview with Yossi Meshulam by Kevin Maney and Michael Damphousse, 2024.

8 | Ready, Set, Go

1. We gathered these videos into a CDA blog post: https://www.categorydesignadvisors.com/how-to-turn-category-design-into-a-video-3-case-studies/.

2. Mike Zani, *The Science of Dream Teams: How Talent Optimization Can Drive Engagement, Productivity, and Happiness* (McGraw Hill, 2021).

3. "Rebooting the Arsenal of Democracy: Anduril Mission Statement," Aduril.com, June 6, 2022, https://blog.anduril.com/rebooting-the-arsenal-of-democracy-anduril-mission-document-67fdbf442799.

4. In *Play Bigger*, the concept is first introduced on page 138.

5. Gail Moody-Byrd, "Constructing Deep Sales: Three Keys to a Successful LinkedIn Takeover," LinkedIn.com, April 19, 2023, https://www.linkedin.com/pulse/constructing-deep-sales-three-keys-successful-gail-moody-byrd/.

6. "How a Gartner Analyst Looks at Categories," *Category Thinkers*, podcast, episode 32, January 23, 2024, https://www.categorythinkers.com/podcast/how-a-gartner-analyst-looks-at-categories.

Notes

9 | Dominant Design Is Everything

1. Kevin Maney, "Ode to Zamboni," *Front Row Seat for a Revolution*, April 17, 2023, https://kevinmaney.substack.com/p/ode-to-zamboni.

2. "Evolution of the Zamboni Ice Resurfacer," Zamboni.com, https://zamboni.com/wp-content/uploads/2020/01/EvolutionofZamboni Machine_web.pdf.

10 | DIY Category Design

1. This section derives from Kevin Maney's "OK Go, YouTube and the Adjacent Possible," *Front Row Seat for a Revolution*, February 22, 2025, https://kevinmaney.substack.com/p/ok-go-youtube-and-the-adjacent-possible.

2. Kevin Maney, "Blend of Old, New Media Launched OK Go," *USA Today*, November 28, 2006.